THE COURAGE SHARE

Also by Ben Crawford

How I Went From Waiting Tables to Being a Professional Blackjack Player (on Accident)

The 29 Minute Card Counting Book

UNLEASH YOUR FAMILY: Chaos to Creativity in One Week

2,000 Miles Together: The Story of the Largest Family to Hike the Appalachian Trail

THE COURAGE TO SHARE

ESCAPING A CULT, FINDING VOICE, BUILDING COMMUNITY

BEN CRAWFORD

FFT PRESS

COPYRIGHT © 2024 Ben Crawford
All rights reserved.
Cover design by D.J. Hansen Design
Print Layout by D.J. Hansen Design

The Courage to Share
Escaping a Cult, Finding Voice, Building Community

ISBN: 979-8-9903447-1-6

for
Kami

"I had so much to say and no one to listen"

Jerry Maguire

1: Preaching
Sharing's antithesis

Danger

I caught my first child, Dove, when she was born in the water after three days of labor. My brother-in-law, Jeremiah, her uncle *and* my spiritual mentor, was sitting at the kitchen table in our tiny apartment two days after her birth. "She's beautiful," he said. My wife Kami and I were both beaming. We couldn't believe we had a baby! She was perfect.

"But you made a big mistake," Jeremiah said.

As long as I can remember I have wanted to share. Milkshakes, movie nights, sunsets and stories. It didn't matter. The second I experienced joy, my first question was who could I share it with? For me, sharing felt as natural as breathing.

My wife was a good sport and went along with most of my ideas - one of which was inviting an 8-person audience to our birth. Having been my first, I underestimated a natural delivery's rawness. The primal screaming, the blood and tears, boobs everywhere…and the stitches - the eight people we had invited had seen everything.

"Our father has spent a lifetime protecting his daughter's dignity and you haphazardly threw it all away in one day," Jeremiah whispered. He wore his usual white t-shirt and khaki cargo pants with a flannel tied around his waist. Across the table, his head was hanging with disappointment.

I respected Jeremiah more than any person in my life. He had been to seminaries around the world and was a shining example of what dedication and living out our faith could look like.

He had two degrees and was a youth pastor. Not the most fashionable, but he didn't care. His priorities were on more important things.

I didn't want to do anything wrong that would offend God or my family. I wanted to be a good brother-in- law, parent and husband. I wanted to be loyal, obedient, and have faith that God would be in control, not me. I valued his words more than anything. And now, his words woke me up like a slap in the face. The burden of my failure, having let down my wife, my family, my mentor and my God, hit me. I had shared too much.
That day, sitting at our kitchen table, I learned a valuable lesson: sharing was dangerous and if not done properly could damage those around you. I knew I had to change. I wanted to connect with, inspire, and help others, but if I was going to do that I needed to find a different way.

Fifteen years later, Kami and I would broadcast our sixth child's birth on the internet, millions would see it and hundreds of people would share that our video changed their lives. We would be bold and proud and confident, and we would lose all of our friends and many of our family members in the process.

But we were not there yet. Right now, we were scared, defeated, and unsure of ourselves.

This is the story of how we discovered our voice, got the courage to share it, and found the people who would support us along the way.

Salvation

As displayed in Dove's birth debacle, my decision-making was flawed. In our Christian home there was a simple reason given: sin. Sin was the problem we were all born with. It meant we were bad at our core. When left alone to our own devices, we would make decisions that hurt others and ourselves.

My experience validated this. As a child, every time I just cut loose and did what I wanted or said what naturally came to my mind, I got in trouble. Pride was the original and most dangerous sin. Humans were the source of pride and I believed everything that came out of us was bad. Sin was also the reason we believed in hell — the place sinners had to go because God could not be near sin.

The only possible solution for sin was to accept Jesus (the only non-sinner) into my heart. And so, in our two-bedroom house with a big picture window in the living room, at the age of four and with my mother's help, I prayed:

> *Jesus,*
> *I confess I am a sinner.*
> *Thank you for dying for my sins.*
> *I want you to come into my heart and save me so*
> *I can be with you in heaven forever.*
> *Amen*

Accepting Jesus Christ into my heart "as my Savior" meant my sin and all the things I got in trouble for were forgiven. This also meant I could go to heaven instead of burning in hell forever. When my dad came home that day, he gave me a hug. He had a huge smile on his face. That Sunday we went to the same church we went to every Sunday, but this week the stained glass and padded wood pews felt different. It felt like home.

Everyone at church was overjoyed at the news of my salvation. They were all going to heaven, too. We were brothers and sisters in Christ now. We were family. We would love each other unconditionally forever. I was in. A few years later, when I was baptized, a line of people stood waiting to congratulate me like I had just graduated from a prestigious university. The Bible was clear: once you had your salvation you could never lose it. It felt so good to be surrounded by others who were saved, knowing we would never have to say goodbye, ever.

In the Christian world, where you were going when you died meant everything. Those going to heaven were called "saved." Being "saved" provided hope and identity, and was supposed to define all of our actions. Instead of doctors or policemen or Americans, we were taught to see ourselves primarily as Christians – chosen and loved by God. Instead of feeling stress or failure, we were supposed to feel victory over the fact that no matter how bad things seemed, we were going to be with God forever in a place where streets are made of gold.

Accepting Jesus into my heart was the most celebrated decision of my childhood. I had never seen my parents so proud. I felt incredible peace. But that peace came with a few strings attached. Anyone who wasn't "saved" we called "lost." And it was my job, I was taught, to tell these "lost" people about Jesus so that they could experience peace and not burn in hell forever.

This made every minute I had, every penny I spent, and every word that came out of my mouth, literally life or death. I decided to follow all of the rules and dedicate my life to helping others feel the peace that I felt. I dreamed of someday becoming an author where I would write about complex ideas and weave stories together in a way that saved people.

I was a passionate child who longed for connection. Since I was taught everything about myself was sinful, the only way I knew to connect with others was by talking about the ideas I had learned in church. Ideas that explained God, removed sin, and showed us how to live well.

For three decades, I dedicated my life to preaching these ideas. Preaching was supposed to prove my significance and help me connect with others. Preaching was supposed to make the world a better place. At least that's what I was told.

The only problem?

It didn't work.

Commitment

No matter what method I had tried, I hadn't converted anyone. A teenager now, clearly failing at my life's purpose, I concluded I needed to put in more effort. I was already going to church every Sunday, often twice, and went to Bible camp in the summer. How else could I show commitment? Find a mentor.

In my evangelical Christian community, mentors were always someone of the same sex with whom you could discuss important life decisions. Because we trusted God (and not our sinful selves), we could demonstrate this trust by obeying and submitting to the authority of a mentor, receiving instruction and often permission in many areas of our lives.

I met my mentor, Jeremiah, in a month-long program called *Training In Christian Living* at a summer Bible camp, three years before I married his sister, Kami. He wore the same cargo pants and white t-shirt all month except on the hottest of days when he would swap out the khaki cargo pants for cargo shorts. He said that you couldn't just accept Jesus as your Savior. You also needed to accept him as your Lord. This meant he owned every part of you. Jeremiah said this commitment is what separated the real Christians from the fake Christians.

Jeremiah was super smart and had Biblical answers for everything. I wanted to be a real Christian. So, at 16, I dedicated everything in my life to God. I burned all of my "secular music" replacing it with Christian music. I read Christian books with titles like *No Compromise*. I mocked things like entertainment, fashion, luxury, and comfort, believing that these were all lesser desires. The only true desire was to love and obey God.

Some Christians put a Christian fish on their car as a proclamation of faith and commitment. I put two fish on our family's white Chrysler minivan. And on my 18th birthday, I got the fish tattooed on my ankle. After the fish tattoo, there was a cross, a dove, a trinity symbol, a heart being washed in blood, Bible verses, lines from the curriculum Jeremiah had invented, and a huge chest piece that celebrated a religious holiday. Each tattoo symbolized my unwavering commitment to share the message of a God that required full faith. Just like my faith, each tattoo was permanent and irreversible. I would have them until the day I died.

My goal was to spend every minute, thought, and dollar of my life trying to convert others. After all, none of it belonged to me. It belonged to God. While my peers spent their evenings making out and watching MTV's Real World, I went to every youth group event – often three nights a week, staying up until 3 a.m. to finish my homework. On weekends I volunteered at all-nighters, where free pizza was offered to lure the unsaved. During spring break, instead of partying, I went on mission trips to Mexico, Ukraine, and Costa Rica. Even though I was in a highly accelerated school and qualified for all honors classes, instead of pursuing law, medicine or money like my peers, I pursued a life in ministry. Later, in the peak of my fanaticism, I would give away our house to my best friend because I had heard God tell me to.

People who were the most committed to God worked at churches. They had given up their careers and all other worldly goals to help the church (His people) and to spread salvation. For me, even this wasn't enough. I committed myself to the goal of a life of poverty as a missionary in Africa. In the ultimate act of commitment, I dreamed of getting shot down in an airplane over restricted air space delivering the gospel to places it had been outlawed. I was willing to give up my life to help people the only way I knew how – by preaching about God.

Conversations With T-Shirts

Before becoming a martyr in Africa, though, I had to deal with high school. In church we were taught that people would approach us Christians and ask why we were so happy. Then we could tell them about Jesus.

But these conversations weren't happening for me. I decided to speed up the process. While my peers wore trendy clothes featuring Quicksilver or No Fear logos, I turned every square inch of real estate on my body into a billboard for Jesus. Every shirt I wore had a Christian message designed to convert. My favorite one said *His Pain, Your Gain* and had a picture of Jesus bench pressing a cross. Another one said in bold neon lettering: *Life's Hard, Pray Harder*. People made fun of me but I didn't care. I cared about people's souls more than even they did, I told myself. I would just be obedient and wait for the conversations to happen.

But no one ever asked me about my shirts. In fact, people actually seemed to avoid my help.

The only conversation I ever had was with our class valedictorian, soccer prodigy, and future medical doctor, Daniel Chun. Daniel Chun had neatly trimmed black hair, thin wire glasses and always wore plain t-shirts with no graphics, sweat shorts that ended right above his knees, and Adidas black leather soccer shoes. One day, when I was wearing a particularly graphic shirt that said: *Actions speak louder than words* and had a picture of Jesus hanging on the cross with a nail stuck through his hand and a close-up of his face in excruciating pain, Daniel, who was also a Christian, pulled me aside and said, "Don't you think you're being a little extreme? I think you should take a more moderate approach."

"The Christian message *is* extreme," I said back. Comments like this were typical of those Christians who were not willing to give up their entire life to the Lordship of Christ and do whatever it took to save people. Jeremiah had warned me about fake Christians like Daniel. Mistaking fanaticism for courage, I used Daniel's feedback as an indicator I was on the right track.

Pathway To Loneliness

When the t-shirt experiment failed and the internet came out, I applied this same mindset of ignoring trends and blasting truth to social media and blogging. I invested hours writing hundreds of blog posts hoping to help people and change their lives forever. I scoffed at those who wrote about humor or finances or anything else popular, believing it was more important to warn people about the danger of burning in hell and offer up my life-saving solution.

My writing got the same result as the t-shirts. At best, I got 1-2 comments, usually from a friend who already believed the same things I did. Even though this lifestyle was all-consuming, I knew it would all be worth it if one person was saved.

Willing to try any medium, I started a YouTube channel. I posted videos of our family sitting around happily eating waffles so I could tell viewers about Jesus. No one was interested. The only questions I got were from people who wanted my waffle recipe.

Over three decades of earnest evangelizing, I hadn't converted, convinced, or helped anyone. Not only was no one getting saved, my methods were having the opposite effect. Everyone hated me. Instead of starting conversations, people avoided me. Instead of being thankful, people looked at the way I was sacrificing myself and concluded I was a pious asshole. At work I wasn't invited to the cool conversations, and I found it impossible to make non-Christian friends. No one would invite me to parties because me and my "help" were a buzzkill.

When people asked for my waffle recipe, I considered them shallow. When people didn't agree with my preaching, instead of examining my methods, I told myself that these people didn't care about the Truth. I told myself I didn't need these relationships and all that mattered was what God thought about me but deep down, I was lonely.

Getting Qualified

When my methods didn't save anyone, I knew it was not for lack of effort. I turned to titans of our faith like Billy Graham and the pastor at our southern California megachurch, who captivated thousands with their eloquent words, and concluded I was under-qualified. Under these seasoned pros, people were getting saved left and right. They had spent years studying the Bible and polishing their methods. I would do the same.

I started memorizing verses, taping them all over the walls of my room. Eventually, I moved to chapters. During the summers, while other kids were relaxing by the pool, I volunteered at a Bible camp in Washington, washing toilets, doing dishes, and going to two Bible studies a day.

It was at this Bible camp at the age of 14 that I met a girl named Kami. She was cute, had sandy brown, medium-length hair, dressed like a tomboy and lived in Washington, two states north of where I was in California. She carried her Bible with her everywhere and seemed as committed to God as I was. I had an instant crush. Over the next four years, I wrote 30 letters to her. She only wrote back three times but I saved each letter. Going to Bible camp where I could study God's word and see Kami became the highlight of my teen years.

Back home in California, during the school year, I took seminary classes offered by the church. I was the only kid there. Committed Christians talked about reading the Bible in a year. I did it in a month. I accumulated bookshelves full of texts all meticulously underlined, studied Greek and Hebrew, went to Bible College, and eventually spent thousands of dollars on tours of the Holy Land to study the original locations of these life-changing events

- anything I could do to make me more qualified to share God with others.

When it came to intelligence and communication, I was often the most qualified in the room. I was a smart kid with an above-average IQ. Later on in my life, I would help billion dollar tech companies explain complex ideas. I passionately cared about people and wanted so badly to help save them from eternal damnation. My blog posts were logical, and my video editing was snappy. I had the product - eternal life with God in heaven. I had everything I needed to help people, but it wasn't enough. All of the people I expected to beg me for answers about how they could get to heaven didn't exist, or at least I couldn't find them. The other Christians around me had similar results.

No matter how much we believed, how much we cared, or how hard we tried, it never helped anyone. Now I know why. It was all preaching.

<u>Preaching</u>

We were told that the only reason people outside of the church were not Christians was because they were ignorant. They didn't know the gospel and someone had to tell them. I did this the only way I knew to communicate: the way Christians talked to each other and the way I had been trained to speak to the world. Although the method came in different packages, underneath, it was all the same: it was preaching.

Preaching, in its many forms, focuses on the message. My message was that Jesus died for your sins and you should accept him into your life and do what He tells you to do. We spent all of our time talking about this message. How it was delivered was not important. Who delivered it didn't matter.

The messenger was flawed and sinful. I was ashamed of myself and my opinions. The best thing I could do for the world was to hide my feelings, vulnerabilities, and experiences and focus on preaching God's message. Our message was called the Gospel - which meant "the Good News" which was supposed to be appealing. All we had to do was deliver it.

I believed in the message of Jesus 110%. I had to. If I didn't, I was going to hell. And while preaching required some bravery because most people disagreed, it did not require any vulnerability. When people disagreed, it wasn't me or my message they disagreed with. They were disagreeing with God and the Bible.

I was good at preaching. I had learned all the methods. I sounded sophisticated, wove ideas together and spoke with conviction. But no matter how hard I preached, I never changed anyone's mind.

<u>Preaching Comes From Superiority</u>

Because my whole life revolved around preaching, I separated the world into two categories: Christians who agreed with my message and non-Christians who believed anything different. Non-Christians had chosen hell. They cared about themselves, not God. They were basically a different species. We didn't call non-Christians inferior. We were more subtle. We called them worldly, sinful, or lost, but our actions revealed our true belief.

We Christians did not respect the opinions of non-Christians on any serious matter. Sure we would let a non-Christian fix our plumbing if we couldn't find a Christian to do it. But when it came to their opinions on raising kids, right or wrong, or anything philosophical, forget about it. Would you trust someone who had chosen to burn forever? I had the answer about how to get to heaven. This meant that since I was four, I believed I had the answers for how every non-Christian should live their life.

I thought I did a good job at covering up this air of superiority but those around me could see through it. I wasn't curious about what any non-Christians thought or how they saw the world. Just like any good salesman, I might listen or pretend to care, but only to get to my punchline to deliver my message, to sell them salvation.

What I didn't realize is that believing you know how others should live is *always* condescending and ostracizing. Preaching always comes from a pedestal and tells people how they *should* live or what they *should* believe as if you know what is best for their lives. Regardless of intention, preaching creates superiority, separation, and coercion. Preaching puts people on different levels and it was making me unrelatable.

This was really frustrating because I wanted nothing more than to help people, have friends, and experience intimacy with others. But the only tool I knew – preaching – was making friendship impossible.

Advice

Everyone preaches about something. While my message was religious, others preached about politics, diet, finances and CrossFit. Preaching happens anytime one person has an idea for how others should live. Preaching is a mindset, and most of it doesn't happen in churches on Sundays. Most preaching comes in the form of giving advice. Unsolicited advice may sound friendly, but any time you tell others how to live, it's preaching.

Advice happens everywhere: between friends, from a boss to an employee, from parents to children or even between lovers. Giving advice for living was all I knew. Regardless of the topic, everything I could think to write about was just giving advice. While each post took the form of a hot take, rant, and a how-to about parenting or out-of-the-box living, behind it all, I was just telling people what to do.

Many people justify giving advice by saying they're trying to help. But the advice giving usually helps the one giving it far more than the one receiving it, regardless of motive. In this way, giving advice was a one-way street, showing that I was the one with the answers. I was always the helper. I never listened to the advice of non-Christians. What I didn't know is that they were not listening to me. My blog posts never convinced or converted anyone and I was more confused than ever.

__Why Preaching?__

Modern Christian art is ridiculed by outsiders. Christian music is mocked and evangelistic movies like the *God's Not Dead* film series are laughable to anyone outside the fold. Many Christians, like me, were smart, well-employed communicators. Why didn't our message resonate?

My answer to why Christians are ineffective and ostracize people with their preaching came to me in Boone County, Kentucky at the Creation Museum. In my 30's, with a booming business and at the peak of the Christian reputation that I had built for myself, we moved our entire family across the country to be where the action was. Living away from the West Coast for the first time, Kami and I found ourselves in the middle of the Bible Belt, just 15 minutes from the Creation Museum – a 75,000 sq. ft. structure that cost 30 million. For an investment this large that claims a goal of "evangelistic outreach" you'd think the intention to effectively communicate with others would be higher than ever. Wrong.

It took me two hours to walk through this collection of dinosaur displays, life-sized dioramas, pro-life exhibits, as well as a depiction of an inner city riddled with crime that serves as a warning for those who do not accept Jesus. The only people in the "museum" were conservative denim-skirt wearing homeschool families that already believed in the Biblical message. There were no unbelievers to be found anywhere. It wasn't hard to see why. The language and methods found within the museum were not only unhelpful to people with different beliefs, but offensive.

The Creation Museum's builders did not lack knowledge or skill, but honesty. When I wore Christian shirts, I thought it was to preach to the lost souls, but really I was preaching to myself. I wore the shirts to display my commitment to God, not for the people I claimed to love. Because of my insecurity, the t-shirts preached a message that I needed to hear, not that the unsaved wanted to hear. The Creation Museum was built for the same reason, and frequented by people who already believed everything it proclaimed. This is also why *God's Not Dead* was played in churches and youth groups but never at an Atheist Club.

My beliefs were fragile and didn't help anyone on the outside. Giving advice reinforced my ego and seeing my beliefs shared on the internet made them seem more valid. In the church, others applauded my preaching. They called me bold and courageous because my words affirmed their life choices. These affirmations, and our preaching, codified our shared ideas and beliefs and made us more impervious to the dissenting outside opinions that we saw as opposition (or even persecution, placing ourselves in the role of victim).

Even though preaching was my only tool, my sheer amount of effort along with financial success was about to lead to a lucky break.

Who I blamed When It Didn't Work

My dream of becoming an author had only intensified as my longing to help people increased. I had practiced my writing on hundreds of blog posts, spent months gathering notes and weekends staring at a keyboard in isolated cabins to etch out a manuscript that I was sure could help people. Finally, a published author saw me speak at a church and said they would introduce me to their agent from New York. My hard work had paid off. The agent gave me all sorts of helpful feedback and walked me through the steps I would need to take to create a proposal and provided me with a sample that would ensure my success.

But my fear of honesty, my overconfidence in preaching my ideas, and my inability to listen would follow me wherever I went. It wasn't that I didn't care, I just had no idea how to think in a different way. When preaching, I didn't assess my audience's acknowledgement or feelings to determine effectiveness or success. The only thing I considered was my level of sacrifice. I saw my preaching (or delivering the gospel) as doing my audience a favor, which meant they owed me. By that measurement, this book would be a smashing success. I doubled down on my sacrifice and for twelve months I read books, scheduled retreats, and battled with myself for endless hours in the office to get the words on paper and finish my proposal.

When the agent got my proposal she said it was terrible and that it wouldn't help anyone. She said the story wasn't compelling and I hadn't taken direction from her. She was not willing to be my agent. She offered a lot of feedback about why the manuscript wasn't working but I didn't read it.

To deal with this criticism I did the same thing I did when my preaching didn't convert anyone. I blamed my audience. I said their hearts were hard or they weren't ready. In my mind, my loneliness and lack of connection was their fault. They felt arrogance. I called it love. With my agent, I figured she simply didn't understand how good my book really was.

At one point I had written off everyone on the entire continent of North America as being close-minded and hard-hearted. I was told that people in Africa would be more receptive to the gospel. This was just another excuse to avoid facing the facts. I had no idea how to connect with people because I was unable to listen.

Not only did I not listen to those who were "lost", I didn't listen to myself. Any fears, conflicting feelings, or desires that didn't line up with the Bible, I simply ignored. I needed to stay focused on what I knew. When something didn't line up, I blocked out the dissonance and spoke louder. I stuck more verses on my wall and thought about heaven.

By not listening or taking feedback, I had cut off my ability to improve as an author or friend. As I moved into my late thirties, I attracted people who spoke weirder and bolder truths, becoming even more fundamentalist. These people listened even less than I did which I interpreted as courageous. Everyone who believed differently was seen as the enemy. Every differing idea was a threat. Everyone was lost. Only we select few had the answer. This us and them mentality made connection impossible.

No place was this more evident than with my kids.

Learning The Hard Way

The hierarchical nature of preaching meant that Christians, who had *the Truth*, are at the top. Everyone else is underneath. Within the Christian group there are other hierarchies, especially within the family. As parents, Kami and I became shining examples of this hierarchy.

At the height of my preaching, parenting was a one-way transaction with me being the dispenser of wisdom and my children being the recipients. This was not an equal playing field and the words we used showed the value that Kami and I placed on our wisdom. Children were actually called fools and it was our job to change them. The roles were strict and rejecting them meant rejecting God's order.

Calling it teaching, we preached in every category of godly living including but not limited to: education, discipline, and relationships. Our entire parent-child relationship was defined by the answers we had that our kids didn't. In our Christian community, parents were ranked by how much effort they put into parenting and how their kids turned out. Parents whose kids behaved well, got married (male and female only), had kids, and stayed inside the church were seen as a success.

In our early parenting years, we experienced a lot of "success." Other Christian parents admired our unique methods and unyielding effort. Many parents were content to send their kids to public schools, but we saw this as a missed opportunity for more time to teach (preach) along with evenings and vacations. Not content with Sunday School, we met in our home for an hour two nights a week to read through the Bible and offer feedback about how the kids should live. We also had structured times on weekends, before and during meals, even pausing movies as an opportunity to teach the kids about what they should and shouldn't do. It felt like a full-time job with no time off, but we knew godly living was important and preaching at our kids was the only way we knew to relate to them.

Like most of the kids in our community, our kids were quiet and obedient, which we took as agreement. But this is like assuming that people pay their taxes because they love the government. The truth was our kids did not feel safe to disagree. They were scared. We had created an environment where there was no space to explore individual ideas, and disagreement or lack of obedience was seen as pride, rebellion, or sin. For disagreement, there were no valid excuses, no healthy dialogue or exchange, only a one-way flow of wisdom from the parents to the kids.

When our kids didn't comply, we used punishment to get our message across. When that didn't work we used emotional isolation. Starting when they were young, we used time-outs where the kids sat alone to contemplate their lack of self-control and when they got older, we grounded them from their peers and emotionally withdrew, blaming them for making bad choices. We called all of this "love" and said that we were just the messengers of truth. We said, "they're gonna have to learn 'the hard way'." Saying "they were gonna have to learn the hard way" was just another way of saying "you're wrong and I'm right and I hope bad things happen to you." We said this same thing to anyone who didn't listen to our preaching about getting into heaven.

As our kids got older, they came to resent our advice. Telling them how bad it was to sneak candy, computer time, or sleeping in wasn't helping them. The advice just created shame and made them feel worse. Instead of coming to us, they were afraid and hid their behavior and true desires. When we did catch them and had the energy to "parent," we turned to the only tools in our tool belt: preach, punish, and shame. Lather, rinse, repeat.

Saying that non-Christians or my kids would someday learn "the hard way" was something we said so we didn't have to face the fact that no one was actually interested in what we had to offer. Had I paid attention to the evidence of what was actually learned "the hard way", I would have seen that no group of people would come back and apologize, say I was right, and profusely thank me for my preaching and moral code. In fact, the opposite was happening. The kids were learning to stay away from us and were on track to hate me.

What Did My Kids Need?

What did my kids want? What did they really need? It wasn't advice. I was giving *them* advice for *myself*. I continued to cram it down their throats, telling myself (just like the people at the Creation Museum) that I was helping.

What my kids really wanted was me but I wasn't giving that to them. I had good reason. Many of the things they were getting punished for, like sneaking around, failing at goals… I was still doing. Believing it was good parenting, I hid weakness from my kids and modeled strength.

Our kids didn't need to know our sins and weaknesses, Kami and I told each other. This would just undermine the message we were giving them. We were supposed to be their models and heroes.

The truth, I would come to understand, was quite the contrary.

2: The Double Life
Fake Sharing

Exile

At church, we believed the minute we were saved and Jesus entered into our hearts, we were a "new creation." "The old has gone and the new has come," we would say. We literally were not the same bad people we used to be. This transformation was key to the message we preached. The joy, the freedom from lustful desires, and the general sense of peace were all things we promised if one followed Jesus. Our lives were the sales pitch.

The problem was, not everything changed the minute I accepted Jesus into my heart. When I was four, I smashed all the peaches off the tree in our front yard with a stick. My dad came home and asked me who did it. Like an idiot, I confessed. My ass hurt for hours. So when my mom caught me sneaking candy, I lied because I didn't want my ass beat. My mom gave me another opportunity to tell the truth. But instead of telling her the truth, I doubled down and told myself it never happened. I saw no benefit from sharing the truth, only consequences. Instead of telling the truth, I spent my energy figuring out how not to get caught. So began a life-long split between what I really thought and what I projected. The older I got the more difficult it became to tell these worlds apart. Creating an alternate reality created confusion inside myself but it was the only solution I knew.

Sure, parents and Sunday school teachers said it was better to be honest. But, if I actually said that the lady at the grocery store was fat, that what mom made for dinner was gross, or that stealing was fun, I got my ass beat. So while there were some rules like "tell the truth" that were important, I learned there were other unwritten rules that were more important.

In church I saw what happened to people who didn't follow these rules - the black sheep. Eventually they just disappeared. I didn't think much of it when it happened to others. In 5th grade, my brother was shipped off two states away to live with my military uncle in the sticks because he was rebellious. So when I was threatened to be sent to a ranch for stealing, I knew my parents weren't bluffing. We even toured the ranch whose mission stated that by introducing us to Jesus Christ (through manual labor) we would have the foundation to be carried through all of life's struggles and successes. I swore I would stop stealing. But no matter how many Bible verses I memorized, how much I went to church, or how hard I preached, I couldn't stop. I just got better at hiding it because I didn't want to be sent to the ranch.

I was confused. I had accepted Jesus into my heart. I was a new creation. I went to church and sang the songs and wanted to make God happy, why wasn't I able to live free from sin like those around me? It didn't matter. Ranch life wasn't for me. I made a clear plan. Stick to the script! If you want to be accepted, hold your cards close to your chest. If you want to be accepted, keep the nasty stuff hidden and stay quiet about it.

Confessions

There was a major contradiction with us Christians projecting perfect lives. The Bible that we based our lives on had all of these pesky verses saying Christians actually *weren't* better than others. The point of the gospel was to focus on God and His grace, not our actions. The Bible was clear that *all* humans were broken sinners. Our motto, as displayed on the popular bumper sticker, was *Christians aren't perfect, just forgiven.* The need for a bumper sticker declaring that one is not perfect shows that there was an expectation that one was. And so, to remain humble we had confession: a time where each person could openly and honestly declare their shortcomings - proving that it was, in fact, God's grace we depended on.

The problem was that to confess anything of substance - to be too dependent upon the grace of God, would mean losing the respect of the community. For this, there was a common workaround. At church the only confessions we made were confessions of the past. The legendary comedian Mitch Hedberg had a famous one liner:

"I used to do drugs.

[pause]

I still do, but I used to, too."

Confessions of the past are easy. By admitting something from the past, we could maintain the narrative that we were healed from sinful desires, that Jesus had fixed us. Hedberg's joke reveals the power of misdirection. By focusing on the past, we didn't have to fully disclose the present…it wasn't a *complete* lie, we told ourselves.

At church, any rule breaking, struggles, or failures were always talked about in the past tense - before we found Jesus. We never talked about current failures which led me to believe that no one around me had any. The problem was, while following rules seemed so easy to others, for me, it wasn't.

Two Worlds

One day, my six-year-old son snuck some candy. I spanked him. Instead of learning and being thankful, he responded by crying —something that had never been acceptable in our house. I saw this as a sign of rebellion and a failure as a parent trying to teach him the dangers of disobedience. In a flash of fury and shame, I slapped him across the face. The rest is a blur except I remember picking him up and Kami says she remembers seeing his blood on the wall. I did this all while believing I was a "new creation" full of the Holy Spirit, whose attributes I had memorized as being "love, joy, peace, patience, kindness, gentleness, faithfulness, and self-control." While abusing my son, I was unable to see any contradiction in what I believed and my actions.

My life was a series of contradictions that were getting worse over time. I cared for people deeply and yet beat them over the head with messages that continually hurt them. I claimed to be loving and non-judgmental, yet with one question, I determined someone's value. I claimed to follow a God that had the power to make us new and take away our sin, yet I would sin more than anyone I knew. I found tasks like reading the Bible and prayer boring and took this as a sign that I didn't really love God.

In church there was a massive emphasis placed on words and appearance. If you *talked* about prayer and holiness, it didn't really matter if you actually *did it*. Fitting in meant faking it till you made it. We talked about how much we loved making God happy, how much we loved His rules and how much peace we gained from following them. There was no space for any conflicting beliefs or stories. We glossed over the aspects of life that didn't fit this narrative and constantly projected positivity and faith. Everything negative was swept under the rug. We focused so much on the positive, we didn't even realize it was fake. Most Christians, including myself, didn't even know to deny or hide this discrepancy because we were not even aware of it. It all happened on a subconscious level. This type of double living was all I had ever known. It wasn't a choice; it was survival.

At first, all my energy was focused on how I appeared as an individual, but eventually, the appearance of my marriage and finances was added to the equation. I had gotten good at hiding things that got me in trouble so suppressing myself and playing the role of one who had a perfect marriage and effortless career came naturally. What I hid changed from stealing baseball cards to sneaking porn to a dysfunctional honeymoon and marriage, but secrets were always my companion. With appearances, nothing was more important than how well-behaved children were. And while people at church loved complimenting and admiring well-behaved children, we spent very little time talking about what it took to get them well-behaved.

Behind every well-behaved child was a lot of strictness and some very nitty-gritty methods that were never discussed. My secrets about parenting practices felt trivial. It was kind of like going to the bathroom, where everyone did it but we just didn't talk about it. There didn't seem to be much shame around it but if you got caught doing it in public, it would be massively embarrassing. No one talked about forcing kids to eat oatmeal, ignoring a child crying, or pinching a kid's neck at the grocery store to keep them silent before they lost their shit in the produce section. No one discussed what it took to get a child to quietly sit through an entire church service. We never talked about anger, control, or abuse. We just applauded the results.

Being fixated on how our children appeared made our primary job as parents the creation of rules and their enforcement. There were rules about everything from food to bedtime to internet usage. Dating and sex were the strictest. Whatever damage was done to get compliance was just eggs cracked to make an omelet.

The moments of rage, shaking, slapping and blood that happened in parenting was just labeled as discipline or tough love and no one pried for specifics. In both parenting and money, there seemed to be a *don't ask don't tell* policy when it came to the darker side of how things got done. Others seemed content to ooh and ahh at the results and, just like preaching, we all agreed that our intentions were good so any damage done to kids wasn't our problem. Well-behaved children meant inclusion and promotion in this religious bubble which was all I knew and cared about. I equated acceptance and advancement in this ecosystem as a sign of my commitment to God and His love for me. They became impossible to separate. And yet deep down, I struggled with the difference between how I was when no one was looking and what I showed people at church. While I was able to get away with this discrepancy in front of people, at my core, I wondered if my love for God was real. Did I really accept Jesus into my heart? Did stealing mean I was still going to burn in hell? Why didn't the Bible verses I memorized help? God had fixed everyone around me but was I just too broken even for God? Why didn't anyone else struggle in the same way I did? If my kids hated me when they got older was that just another sacrifice I needed to make?

The worst part was the sacrifices I was making weren't helping anyone. They were just an excuse to justify my behavior and mask the painful feelings I had no idea how to face.

I already felt like a monster, but things were about to get worse.

Isolated

Being rejected by a literary agent, scaring away co-workers, and having my kids hate me didn't slow me down. In fact, I took the rejection as a sign I needed to have more courage and speak up and live more boldly. The older I got, the more outspoken I became in my public speaking and writing. This increased the stakes of my secret life being found out and I had to hide more and more. Successful preaching was contingent upon me representing my successful moments and shining light on my achievements. Doing this well distracts people from the dark corners.

But even though others didn't see the dark corners, I knew they were there. I was becoming disappointed in myself. I wasn't the father I wanted to be. I wasn't the husband I projected. I wasn't the honest businessman people saw. Being honest about my fraudulence would mean letting down my kids, spouse, and everyone at church. I pushed any doubt down and pretended it wasn't there. Eventually, I stopped feeling altogether.

Did you catch that last sentence?

I didn't just stop feeling doubt; I didn't feel *anything*. I was numb. I didn't feel joy and was so disconnected from my body I was unable to dance. I didn't even feel sadness. I didn't cry for more than ten years. Even sex became boring as I played porn in my head just to climax.

By ignoring so much reality, my life became a series of platitudes. All I talked about was what I was *supposed* to do, what I was supposed to feel, how I was *supposed* to live. The Bible verses that were posted on my bedroom wall were now on our family's walls and published on Facebook for everyone to see. With every new blog post, my conscious and subconscious grew further apart. I was faking it through life but unfortunately, I wasn't making it. I was alone, frustrated, and desperate for any breakthrough to bridge this gap.

I wanted to feel connection with others.

I wanted to know what was real.

Accountability Group

In Bible college, while Kami and I were still dating, I heard about a men's group to help those who struggled with "sexual purity and lust." I felt hope that maybe I could reconcile the fractured parts of myself and experience connection with others who were similar. The Bible demanded sexual purity and we interpreted this as no sex before marriage. This also meant no porn or masturbation.

Back then, I was a horny college boy with my own computer and the full power of the internet was just being discovered. I constantly felt like a failure and jumped at the offer of the men's group. This was the first time I heard that other Christians struggled after accepting Jesus into their heart. Maybe I wouldn't have to suffer alone.

It was also at Bible college that I had committed to being a missionary in Africa to tell people about Jesus. Missionaries were like the Navy SEALs of Christianity and got the most respect. I wasn't converting any Americans and was willing to sacrifice my comfort for God, so I knew this was for me.

But before becoming a missionary, I had to get this porn habit under control. I couldn't be a spiritual Navy SEAL while sneaking around looking at pictures of naked women that were not my wife. This was seen as cheating — equivalent to adultery.

My first meeting, there were five of us crammed around a tiny kitchen table at 7 a.m. on a Sunday morning. My palms were sweating but I was excited. Jeff, the leader, hung his head and shared. "I dropped the ball this week."

We nodded. I thought about my week trying to download porn using the archaic modem through the college's filtered internet, the shameful masturbation sessions in the shower and the feelings of guilt afterward. We waited to hear the rest of Jeff's story.

"But I repented and talked about it with God and got forgiveness and am super thankful that God says He loves me no matter what." Everyone's head lifted and mumbled positive affirmations of this good news.

This was the accountability group's "sharing formula." The confessions were always quick and vague. More time was spent focusing on the positive list of truths we all already believed should help us overcome our struggles, as if we had all moved on. No one ever offered embarrassing specifics, and no one ever asked any questions.

But this sharing formula didn't change any of my behaviors. This method for dealing with inconsistency became the method I used anytime the ideals that I preached didn't line up with how I was actually living: preach louder and hide the parts that don't align.

These meetings were disappointing but they were all I had. Week after week I went back hoping for more but it was always the same formula. Deep down I wondered if the sense of transparency or connection I wanted was too idealistic or if maybe my sins were just worse than everyone else's and they just didn't have much to confess.

Climbing The Ranks

After Bible College, the year before I got married, I started working at a church. This was a huge spiritual promotion. I was endorsed by those who knew God the best, were the most committed and I was getting paid for it — the perfect stepping stone for my missionary work in Africa.

But I was surprised to find out that church leaders didn't seem the most committed to God. They cared about cable TV and designer clothes just like everyone else. The main difference was that they preached the loudest and seemed the most polished. In other words, they were the ones who were able to hide things the best. My passion misdirected everyone at church from my failures and helped me climb the religious ranks.

I never set out to take advantage of this system but it kept rewarding me for what felt natural. I kept thinking that someday there would be a test where someone would ask me "What do you do in private?" and not let me worm out with vague answers like "dropped the ball" but the test never came. In fact, the more success I achieved, the fewer questions I got. It was don't ask, don't tell to the extreme. We just assumed the best of each other.

More than these small successes of climbing the ranks within the church, I was focused on starting a family. Having a family was the ultimate sign of accomplishment within the church. Besides that, I wanted a group where I could be myself and not have to hide anything. All of this started with finding a spouse. My senior year of high school, my family had moved from California to Washington, and I was now closer to Kami — my Bible camp crush. Since getting Kami's attention by writing letters had been a bust, I thought going to the same Bible study might get her attention, even though it was an hour away. This ended up in a phone conversation in which we both said we "had feelings" for each other. A major victory.

I was excited when, at the Bible study the following Thursday, she said she wanted to talk on the porch privately. "You know how I said I have feelings for you?" she said.

"Yeah" I said, waiting eagerly.

"Well, I just wanted you to know I could never marry you."

The words stung. But they also had the reverse effect of what Kami intended. I was interested in Kami because she wasn't like other girls. While they wore trendy, flashy outfits, Kami wore plain sporty clothes. She wasn't just a tomboy, she was a sexy tomboy. While other girls seemed flirty and boisterous, Kami was quiet and unassuming. And where other people tried to impress by giving answers they thought people wanted to hear, Kami, who felt guilty for leading me on, had delivered her simple truth to me on the deck. She had a steady and simple presence about her, and I wanted more of that in my life.

So, I ignored her words and made myself available at every opportunity, even being the shoulder to cry on when she came back from a mission trip of her own to Italy mourning the loss of her Italian crush. "Best to let these things go," I nobly advised. *Have you considered Africa?*

My persistence worked. Six months later we were a couple. I applied the same all-or-nothing mentality I had used in Christianity to our relationship. I bought an engagement/wedding ring for $229 which was all the money my non-materialistic ass could muster. I went to her parents to ask their permission to marry her. Kami's parents both wore Polo Ralph Lauren, got their hair cut weekly, washed their sheets daily, and always dressed like they were ready for church. This made sense since they both worked at church and her dad was in the military. They said I needed a real job. The $400 a month the church was paying me wasn't enough. Six months later I came back and asked again. This time I had a job working at FedEx getting paid $12 an hour, which I doubt is what they had in mind but by now they realized I was not going away. So they agreed, under the stipulation that I help her get a degree.

On Christmas Day, 1999, walking through Bothell Landing Park, just outside of Seattle, I told Kami I wanted to follow Jesus for the rest of my life and that my life was going to be hard. When that didn't scare her off, I told her I wanted her to follow Jesus with me. Then I pulled out the ring, got down on one knee, and asked her to marry me.

We started planning our wedding right away. We didn't register for gifts, believing that material possessions would just distract us from being missionaries together in Africa. One month later, a week before I turned 21, with all of our parents cautioning that we were too young, we exchanged vows, declaring to love God and each other for the rest of our lives. We were pregnant within a month. I put the missionary gig on hold to help Kami get a nursing degree to make good on my promise to her parents and because that was something that would help us in Africa. In the meantime, we hosted Sunday night dinners for broke college kids and I used what little free time I had making cinnamon rolls for all 200 people at church, paying for the ingredients with my new $12 an hour construction job that I hated. No one I worked with ever smiled, they used the word "cocksucker" to describe everything, and I couldn't relate to anyone's lifestyle.

A year and a half after we had our first child, we gave birth to our second. We put our Africa plans on hold while we waited for Kami to finish school. I left construction and got a job waiting tables at Red Robin. At first I was really excited because people smiled, the work was indoors, and people's vocabulary was more extensive. But making minimum wage at Red Robin wasn't cutting it either so I set my sights on making money for Kami's tuition while being a stay-at-home dad. I found success financially in casinos beating the game of blackjack, in real estate, and in the internet startup world. At first, making money felt like a failure — like I was selling out, not giving everything to God. I had ignored my talent in business because I saw it as lesser than my calling to spread the message of Jesus. I expected, and hoped, that my pastor would call me out for abandoning my true calling.

Instead, he seemed impressed by my new riches from winning at blackjack. "My dad plays craps," he said, and he and his family loved joining us for the free meals at the casino. Now that I had a wife and children and financial success, my status in the church went up. The pastor and elders started coming to me for property and marriage advice and for investment opportunities. I was becoming more trusted, respected, and influential in the church, which only made my secrets seem more and more dangerous. I distracted myself with the acclaim of the people I had dedicated my life to, but deep down I felt trapped.

The $12,000 Lie

The blackjack gig was simple math and I enjoyed it. Ultimately I won enough playing the game to buy a house with granite countertops — something I never thought I would have. This got the attention of a few friends from high school who asked me to teach them how to beat the game.

Eventually four of us created a blackjack team. We combined our money and skill and traveled the country, dressing up in disguises to not get caught by casinos, eating free meals and occasionally playing blackjack for 24 hours straight. Often we played solo, traveling with large amounts of our combined team money. The team was held together by a strong desire to beat casinos and an impenetrable code of moral honesty to regulate the large amounts of cash that were constantly moving around.*

Everything was going great until one sunny day in Woodinville, WA, when Kami and I went to the playground with our kids. As was common, I left the doors of our beat-up, '91 white Honda Civic unlocked. We never kept anything valuable in it. But that day, I had $12,000 worth of cash and casino chips in a blue satchel. The money belonged to our blackjack team.

When I came back to the car, the blue satchel was gone. Someone had stolen it. I felt sick to my stomach. The team policy was clear. The money was my responsibility. I was supposed to report the theft to the team and I would need to pay it back. I did the math — $12,000 would set us back half a year. This was half a year I would be working instead of with my kids. Half a year longer to get to tell people about Jesus in Africa.

---

* *My first two books and the documentary Holy Rollers: The True Story of Card Counting Christians, detail these events.*

But the biggest cost was I would look like an idiot to my friends. They would think I was foolish and irresponsible. I had worked so hard to build my reputation and qualifications in the church and now that was being threatened.

As a kid, it was stealing baseball cards and candy that almost got me sent to the ranch. I assumed that as I got more money, these desires would go away. I had prayed and memorized verses like crazy but nothing had helped.

I was a cheapskate who compulsively took advantage of store's return policies and fudged numbers on documents to get loans forgiven. But the entire foundation of the team depended upon our trust and honesty with each other. I had my dream job with my best friends, didn't want to hurt anyone and knew that if I violated their trust it would end the relationship.

But I was too afraid and in a split second, I made the decision.

I went into evasion mode, coming up with a story to hide the truth. It was familiar territory. Instead of reporting the missing $12,000 to my friends, I would report it as a loss from a casino. This way I wouldn't have to pay it back. I justified it by saying that in the grand scheme of team play, it wouldn't make a huge difference.

Getting caught losing $12,000 was one thing. Getting caught lying about it was another. No one could find out about this, ever. Not even Kami. She was too honest.

So, just like I had done with the candy and baseball cards, I told myself that nothing had happened. But where lying about cards and candy had only created a split within myself, now my need to appear virtuous created separation from the one person who had accepted me — Kami.

The drive home was silent. Kami said "Are you ok? You seem quiet."

"Yeah, I'm fine," I said. I tried hard to believe my words.

Alone At Work

I was able to justify my moral failure by saying I would make the money back up to my friends. I hated to admit it, but I was far better at making money than getting people saved. Starting businesses and making money felt natural and I felt ashamed that I enjoyed it so much. Even though my only education was a year of Bible college, I had built our 4-person blackjack team into more than 30 players, investors, and a management structure that I led with my best friend.

When I got bored of that, I founded an internet startup that used video to tell stories with my mentor and brother-in-law Jeremiah and another friend from Bible camp named John. John was a tall and skinny skater that wore baggy pants in high school. He had brown shaggy hair that he tucked behind his ears and now that he had gotten older, his baggy skater pants had gotten skinnier. Our business retreats were a mix of business strategy, theology discussions about how we wanted to use our money to further the kingdom of God, and cigars and microbrews (the closest to partying our Christian code allowed). I was now being paid by companies like Google and Facebook to make stick figure cartoons but it wasn't all a dream come true. My dream of becoming a writer and helping people had deteriorated into making advertisements for large companies, claiming that their product would make everyone's life better, including gambling companies that I hated. I wasn't proud of my work and was embarrassed to show the videos I had made to any of my friends. My dream of becoming a missionary in Africa was slipping further and further away. Not to mention, Kami had now decided that she hated nursing, what she had gone to school for.

While I was mourning my aborted plans of missions in Africa, those at church were wowed by my big numbers and extravagant lifestyle. People were impressed when I hired a personal assistant to play tennis with my kids. But financial success came with the same price tag as my spiritual success: isolation. No one ever asked me where the money came from, the motivation, or if there were any struggles or dishonest moments. Because I had so much money, I felt guilty talking about it. People with money weren't supposed to complain.

I wanted to make my own videos about topics I cared about but this was selfish and could lead to pride — the most dangerous sin. Humans were sinful and not to be trusted. Their words were inferior to God's word. The cure was to focus on God and His ideas and to serve others. I guess we were supposed to ignore the stacks of money that piled up as a result. My business partner, John, set the gold standard by leaving our company that made advertisements and started making videos that explained the Bible. He was using his gifts the way they were intended — invisibly. His videos featured the Bible and God's ideas for life.

On our weekly phone calls he told me about the famous Christian authors and pastors that were lending their name and support as the project launched a successful kickstarter, raising six figures. Wanting to contribute, I sent a donation of $10,000 to fund the video for the book of Leviticus — one of the more boring books of the Bible. John called to thank me for the money, but more importantly for the friendship. He said if I ever needed help, he was there for me. Even though we were no longer business partners, we would always be friends.

I dreamed of someday making videos but about what? His Bible videos were better than mine ever would be and I couldn't imagine anything else. My internal life was falling apart.

Alone At Home

The isolation that came with professional and social success was difficult to navigate, but nothing compared to the loneliness I felt in my marriage. Since childhood, I had longed for a romantic friend I could share everything with. Abstaining from premarital sex, I had naively assumed that once I was married I would have unlimited sex, which would make any feeling of separation disappear.

But marriage was hard, harder than anything I had imagined, with our sex life being the hardest. We went on our honeymoon during the summer to the small resort town of Whistler in Canada. I had surprised Kami with a condo within walking distance of the village with four bedrooms, jacuzzi tubs, and our own private hot tub. I looked forward to endless amounts of guilt-free sex. Kami, who had spent her teenage years repressed and abused had a different idea. For her, the honeymoon would be less about endless romping and more about unpacking years of trauma.

It all came to a head on the 5th day of our honeymoon — my 21st birthday. I knew how I wanted to celebrate. But instead of cute lingerie, sexy bubble baths, and rabbit-like frequency, Kami said, "I wish I had never gotten married." My whole world unraveled. We spent the next two days and the four hour drive home in complete silence.

I had never heard any married people discuss these struggles and assumed there was something wrong with my marriage and something wrong with me. My mentor, Jeremiah, my business partners, and everyone else at church seemed so happy in their marriages. All they talked about was how good marriage was and how God designed it. No one ever complained.

Deep connection felt impossible. Kami and I fought often, and when we did, I retreated to porn and masturbation, which I believed was cheating. Every cycle brought feelings of defeat, failure and shame. Eventually, I confessed to Kami to alleviate my conscience but kept these cycles a secret from everyone else.

Instead of intimacy, we each focused on playing roles that would just help us get through the day. I made the money and she cleaned the house and fed the kids. We played roles in our intimate relationship, too. I always initiated sex and extended the leadership, and she played the part of a helpless damsel and submissive wife. This was the best way we could relate to each other.

We couldn't understand each other's needs or even our own. Sex was used to alleviate anxiety and bring in a fleeting sense of unity and we both took comfort in the fact that at least we weren't divorced. Instead of breaking patterns, our energy went into making our relationship look good so we would continue to get the esteem and support of the community — we wanted to make God happy.

My inner and outer world were in perpetual conflict. I often felt depressed and crazy. I was celebrated for my success, but I was more hopeless and isolated than ever.

Promotion

To suppress my internal discrepancies, I focused on my increased successes at work, church, and in my family. I was seen as devoted, courageous, and intelligent, and people at church sought out my leadership and advice. During the summer, we still volunteered at Bible camp but now took our whole family, which had expanded to five children. Our kids loved camp as much as we did and returning with our family (especially since it was large) was an indicator of faithfulness and success. Working in the kitchen together at the place we loved became the highlight of our summer.

My hard work of building trust and a reputation was paying off. When not at camp, my calendar was packed with younger men who were begging to meet to ask me questions about business ventures, leadership and family, or even just to get the social clout that came with meeting Ben Crawford. Kami had women who met her at 6 a.m., bringing her coffee and bagels to get her wisdom on being a Christian wife and how to parent our now large family.

Business was also a success. I joined the fanciest health club in town and sat around naked in the steam room with all the rich Microsoft employees. I was attending the largest poker game in Seattle and in 2013, my first year after moving to the midwest, I was voted Ernst & Young Entrepreneur of the Year, where I schmoozed with the region's most prestigious people wearing a rented tuxedo. I was speaking to entrepreneurial groups of thousands, and church leaders offered front row seats to downtown concerts. I was teaching weekly classes to the staff of the largest multi-campus mega church around that claimed to be the fastest growing church on the continent. They all wanted my juice.

Back when we were in Seattle, it came as no surprise when our church offered to promote me to deacon. This designation came with training, a rigorous testing process and would result in my name emblazoned on the weekly church bulletin next to elders and pastors. I wondered if my secrets would come up or be found out.

The thought made me nervous and excited. I didn't feel right living a double life. I had been kept safe by the church's *don't ask, don't tell* policy but if there ever was a time for reckoning, it would be deacon training. I didn't know if I would tell the truth if asked point-blank about stealing or masturbating, but I fantasized about getting caught.

The first training session was at the church office in downtown Seattle, with three other men being considered for the same role. Right after the opening prayer, one of the men announced that he looked at porn, implying that he may also masturbate. Everyone in the circle looked down. I had been in the church for more than 20 years and had never heard anyone confess to a sin this bad, especially someone in leadership. I wondered would he be dismissed and then punished?

Instead, the pastor said, "No one's perfect, everyone makes mistakes." And then, "I don't think it would be helpful for others to know specifics about this."

One Step Forward, Two Steps Back

The pastor's endorsement of secrecy felt like a get-out-of-jail-free card. Maybe I could have all of the benefits of leadership without the shame of being outed…ever. But while being outed was scary, it was the only way I could imagine getting help. While being a deacon felt like the next step of spiritual success, it did not solve my bigger problems:

- I felt disconnected from my closest friends because they didn't know who I really was.

- I always felt one slip up away from being found out, exposed, and exiled.

- I suffered from headaches, lower back pain, and stress from the maintenance of two very separate and conflicting lives.

- My writing, advice, or any other content, stayed at the safe, superficial zone of preaching, unhelpful to anyone on the outside.

Everything I made was boring at best, ostracizing at worst. The only messages I knew how to share were advertisements, both God's and Google's.

I was a holy rolling Don Draper.

<u>Living In Hell</u>

I was an artist. I had out-of-the-box ideas and a unique approach to life that I felt the world needed. But I was constrained by a belief system that made most of my creativity off limits. I took notes furiously, worrying that I was going to forget an idea or that it would be removed from the earth permanently unless I published it. I filled notebook after notebook. Sitting on my shelf, these notebooks collected dust and the ideas got stale. Every day I lost more and more motivation and was not any closer to sharing or publishing. I was nearing my 40th birthday and the best case scenario I could imagine was my kids discovering my journals and publishing them after I died — even though they didn't even know they existed.

So, instead of focusing on my ideas, I went to church every Sunday to focus on God's ideas. I listened to the sermons intently. Even though many were long and boring, I took notes, looking for ways to find connection with God, myself, and others. I started downloading and listening to sermons on other days of the week. More verses, more ideas, more preaching. The more I hung out with people at church, the more shitty I felt. I felt guilty. Like it was my fault. With no ability to talk about my shortcomings, get advice or feel companionship, my unacceptable behaviors got worse, never better. I was avoiding the natural maturity that came with age.

Deep down, I wanted to hear people's deepest darkest secrets and I wanted to share mine. This was intimacy and I longed for it. I wanted to be known and loved for who I really was, not just the role I played.

Even though I knew I was going to heaven, I felt like I was living in hell. My life was controlled by shame. Did I have to wait until heaven where we would have no secrets? Could I make it that long without getting caught?

The discrepancy and hidden lies were killing me. The only thing I knew to give people, advice, was actually driving people away.

I wanted more. I wanted connection.

I needed something else.

3: The Basement
Real Sharing

Sexaholics Anonymous

"And then I climbed back *into* the dumpster an hour later and got the Playboys I had just thrown away. I'm disgusted with myself," said Pierre. He spoke with a thick French accent and worked at the local deli. You could tell because he was wearing his work clothes. For his shift after or from the night before I couldn't tell.

At Bible camp, my cousin Kyle had casually invited me to a Sexaholics Anonymous (SA) meeting. At first, I hesitated. But I had nothing better happening Sunday morning at 7 a.m. Why not check it out and support a family member? What could it hurt being a casual observer?

A week later I walked into a dingy church basement filled with self-proclaimed sexaholics. Unlike the beautiful upstairs sanctuary, a place with stained glass and padded wood pews where parishioners drank artisanal coffee, the sexaholics met in the shitty basement with a low ceiling, fluorescent lighting, metal folding chairs and drank Folgers with N'joy powdered creamer.

The state of the basement reflected the people in it. Some had exposed themselves to strangers, some had cheated on their spouses and lied to their bosses, all to get more sex. And then there was Pierre talking about digging his porn out of the dumpster. I was disgusted. But I was also intrigued.

After Pierre's story, I waited for someone to offer advice or act shocked. But no one said, "Oh, my God!" or walked out. There was no virtue signaling by the crowd, not even a surprised look. Only a kind of quiet nodding that said "been there." As I walked into my regular 10 a.m. church service that morning, where everyone was smiling and talking about how thankful they were that Jesus made their relationships better and saved them from temptation, I realized I had never heard people talk about the shameful parts of themselves. For 30 years, I had only heard about love, belief, faith, and victory.

But this was because those stories were all preaching. And preaching was all I had ever heard, and in turn was all I could offer the world. The sex addicts were doing something different. They talked about their failures, and I wanted to hear more. In that secret society of sex addicts there was something going on I had never heard before: sharing.

Week after week I went back. I heard the same stories. I heard Gina talk about trying to stay off Craigslist. I heard Bob talk about losing his wife and job. I heard Pierre describe his battle with the dumpster. No solutions. No preaching. No advice. Only sharing.

There's Another World Here

The dingy basement was different from anything I had experienced. I felt completely out of place. Even though it was filled with society's derelicts, they had a strict set of rules. My cousin explained them to me.

- **No membership.** At least none that you could earn. Unlike the church, you didn't need to accept Jesus into your heart, live up to a certain standard or agree to any beliefs. All you needed to be a member was a "desire to stop lusting." Since I felt guilty every time I looked at porn, I qualified.

- **No promotion.** 12-step groups such as SA have a strict public relations policy that is based upon "attraction rather than promotion." My Christian upbringing was all about promoting my message with t-shirts, all-nighter events, free pizza, and fancy cinnamon rolls to lure people in. Missionaries were the most extreme form of promotion, taking God's message to the ends of the earth. In SA, not one cent was spent on advertising or promotion. There were no billboards. The message was transmitted a different way.

- **No preaching.** What mattered in SA was the honesty of one's own sharing. Any belief system that wasn't focused on one's own experience was seen as "dissension or distraction" and not permitted. Even obvious statements like "affairs are bad" were left out. They weren't helpful. People didn't talk about others outside the group and they didn't talk about their beliefs. They only shared their own experiences.

With all the new rules, I still didn't understand what was really going on in the basement. At first I felt sorry for everyone with their soiled reputations and shitty coffee but they had something I didn't quite understand.

I needed to know more.

The Share

The biggest difference between the sanctuary and the basement was that instead of a pastor preaching from the front, members of SA spent their time sharing in a circle. In SA, hearing how they *should* live, like we heard in church, did not help. These people knew the rules. And they knew they had failed. Hearing the rules even more just made them feel worse. They needed something stronger than preaching about rules and how things *should* be. They needed to talk about the way things *were*. They needed sharing.

Fifty minutes out of the one hour meeting were spent sharing. People introduced themselves by saying, "I'm Steve, I'm a sexaholic," to which everyone would say, "Hi, Steve." And then Steve would begin his share. The topics people shared varied wildly. But most shares focused on struggles from the previous week. These were not like the confessions from the past that I heard back at church (*I used to do drugs*) where people talked about their sins from two decades ago before they found Jesus. These confessions were from *that* week, sometimes the night before.

Yesterday I was up all night surfing the internet for ways to cheat on my wife.

Three days ago I lost my sobriety, after five years, and now I feel like a failure.

Although it was depressing, the 50 minutes always flew by. Even though I had never dug porn out of a dumpster or tried to meet anyone on Craigslist, it seemed like every story had an element I could relate to; a feeling, pattern, or behavior. It felt like they were sharing something about me.

Back at church, we always ended stories of failure, with success.

I was pissed at my neighbor

but

I love them and now I pray for them.

I got in a fight with my wife

but

I realized I needed to be thankful and we forgave each other.

I used to steal

but

now I don't because I know it's wrong.

All those church stories were tied up in a neat little bow that illustrated the power of Jesus and came with a lesson about how others should live. The stories at the 7 a.m. basement meetings were not tied up in a bow. There was no air of superiority or moral certitude, the very things I thought made someone qualified to speak.

And yet, even without the strength and victory, I constantly felt uplifted and captivated listening to these failures in the basement. Their sharing contained something I had never been exposed to. I couldn't describe it yet, but I needed to figure out what it was.

Elements Of Sharing

As I came back the next week, and then the week after that, I observed what made sharing so different and captivating.

Sharing is real.
The thing we Christians spent all of our energy on — our belief system — was abstract. You can't see beliefs or touch them. SA members shared about *what happened* in their week. It involved real places and body parts, and they described what they were feeling *in the moment*. Not what they wanted to feel but what they actually felt.

Sharing is vulnerable.
Someone could preach that porn is bad. But this tells you nothing about what they did last night. Compared to sharing, preaching was safe. Honest sharing requires vulnerability. In the basement, they shared about the things that make people blush, that would offend some and scare away others — things you wouldn't hear anywhere else. Sharing was risky because it took a part of you that was usually covered up and exposed it so others could see. To me this seemed unimaginable.

Sharing creates connection.
I was so concerned with impressing people I never had deep connections. Preaching puts someone on a pedestal and ostracizes an audience, vulnerable sharing does the opposite. Sharing was a gift that was offered to the group with no agenda to convert them. It gave the group an opportunity to see you. It created an opportunity for connection. People could say "I like that" or even "I don't like that" but now I have someone to talk about it with.

Good Sharing Includes The "Bad" Bits

I always thought I knew how to tell my story but I was just cherry picking the bits I thought the world wanted to hear — the pieces that glorified God and would get people to convert. This wasn't sharing. This was advertising. My life "story" was a piece of manipulative, obsolete, and boring propaganda, a sales pitch for heaven designed to convert others, not one concerned with accuracy.

Sharing is less concerned with the results and more about the accuracy. When truly sharing you do not get to decide *what* you share only *if* you share. Just like you don't get to choose the weather, the color of your eyes, or what continent you are born on, most of what happens in our week (including our emotions) is outside of our control.

Sharing is the decision to take those events and states of being that simply are and to transmit them to another as honestly as possible. Your share is just reporting the news…your personal news. Whether it's rainy or sunny, a good weatherman tells the truth.

While delivering the news sounds easy enough, any news about me, I believed, was sinful, dangerous, and could get me banished. Keeping my news a secret had been my number one priority for the last 30 years and probably one of the reasons I had placed myself in a community that focused on belief. When it came to sharing, I couldn't figure out if everyone in the basement just had way more courage than I did or just had nothing to lose.

As I came back week after week, I wondered what made them different and if I would ever get the courage to share?

The Response

The mystery to how sharing happened in the basement came in what happened *after* a share. At church, when you didn't tie your story up in a neat bow, someone else did it for you. If someone shared about a failure, it was always followed by advice, prayer, a Bible verse, or affirmation of our beliefs. These responses were always couched as loving but were predictably unhelpful. Responses like this reminded me of things I responded to my kids. "I'm so tired."…"Have you thought about going to bed earlier?"

Responses like this were a form of virtue signaling that affirmed a code but did not truly help the one struggling. If someone said "I stole" they got a response in the form of a Bible verse, a book recommendation, or a story of our own success that essentially amounted to "you shouldn't steal." We always overlooked the fact that the person already knew the Bible verses we quoted. Would hearing it again really help?

In the basement, sitting on the metal folding chairs, smelling the stale Folgers, I could see the hidden cost of these responses. Advice was always offered from a position of superiority. And while it may have been five parts help, it also contained 95 parts judgment. The superiority made church an unsafe place to share my truest stories because deep down I feared being judged, or worse, excluded if my story didn't line up with the ideals we repeated beneath those stained-glass windows.

In SA, one rule made it safe to share — *"No Cross Talk." "No Cross Talk"* meant no one was allowed to offer advice, judgment, Bible verses or book recommendations regardless of how helpful the intent. In fact, even sharing a relatable story or affirmation of the story was not allowed.

Instead, after each share, everyone in attendance would simply affirm the speaker by saying, "Thanks, Steve." This would be the crowd's response *every single time*, regardless if Steve shared a success, a failure or even if he cried the entire five minutes.

This type of response said that every person, share, and experience is welcome. It said *that* you shared is more important than *what* you shared. It said your courage, vulnerability, and presence is more important than your expertise. And most importantly it said "No matter what you say, we see you, we hear you, and we're not going anywhere."

Qualifications

My original plan in SA was to build my reputation like I had in the church. I would work harder, be more committed, and use my talents to woo people over. I imagined inviting everyone over to my house for cinnamon rolls where they could see my granite countertops, well-behaved children, and solid marriage so I would have the respect I was used to at church.

But the more I came back, I could see that none of my methods for church successes or clout worked in the basement. At first, I got frustrated with SA and wanted to quit. All of the qualifications I had spent my entire life constructing were thrown out the window. I had nothing to share, nothing to add, and no one respected me.

In SA, qualifications were not based on morality, they were based on honesty. This meant a new person could show up off the street and have the most moving share of anyone in the room. Not because they knew the most or lived the best but because they were desperate, vulnerable, and honest. Even after going to meetings for a year, I still didn't know how to be honest about most of the things in my life.

Those simple words "I'm Ben and I'm a sexaholic" and everything that followed seemed untrue, pointless, and impossible to speak. I didn't feel desperate. I didn't want help. And I didn't know how I could be vulnerable after spending my entire life protecting myself to appear strong.

Acknowledging The Other 50%

My identity came from seeing my life story as a simple three-act play. The first act was terrible: I suffered from sin and was going to hell. In the second act I found a way to end the suffering: I accepted Jesus into my heart, which was the climax. The climax of my life happened when I was four years old. Ever since, I've been in the third act: the victory celebration. Any suffering I felt that seemed to conflict with the "victory" of accepting Jesus was swept under the rug.

I wasn't trying to hide my deepest feelings or darkest experiences, I just didn't even know that they existed. I had been trained to discount my feelings and natural persuasions and I gaslit myself into thinking they weren't important. Being told that what I believed had the power to send me to either heaven or hell made beliefs take precedence over any other aspect of personhood. Feelings of failure were make-believe, something not worth focusing on.

But now in the basement, I just heard people's pain. There was no sweeping it under the rug or ignoring it. It felt like they were living in the climax of their life now. And I started to see that this pain and these failures mattered. They helped people make sense of the past and affected how they acted on a daily basis. Pain was why people did drugs, overspent on their credit card, and even looked at porn. I heard people describe loneliness, emotional pain, and depression. Previously, my only categories of pain were starvation, crucifixion, and getting shot down in an airplane on my way to becoming a martyr (and even *that* was to be considered a joy).

With these new categories I had to rethink my entire life. Now, for the first time, I could see that I had suffered. My entire life I had longed for intimacy and integration. I wanted to live authentically but instead, masked and concealed my true self. I had seen those who lived authentically be branded by the church and kicked out by their family and friends, and so I vowed to keep certain parts of myself hidden to feel safe. As a result, I had shut down and exiled entire parts of myself because they were not welcome. Shutting parts of yourself down for extended periods of time has side effects including depression, anxiety, and my most acute one: isolation.

By focusing on the positive all the time, I lived a pretty hopeless life because at least 50% of the things that happened in my life needed to be hidden and went unacknowledged. My beliefs and solutions only accounted for 50% of my life. Even though it was shocking and depressing at first, by acknowledging my weakness, I felt hope. Fifty percent of my life, my activities and myself were being acknowledged for the first time. Maybe, if there was a God, He was big enough to love all of me…but what about other humans? Could they love me?

Finding Connection

They say "it's lonely at the top" because expertise brings isolation. In an ecosystem that ranks you according to performance, I had tried to distinguish myself from others my entire life. I was Ben the non-partier, or Ben the millionaire and even to those inside the church I was Ben the missionary, or Ben the committed. Pursuing expertise in religion turns everyone else into competition.

In this way, my success in business and in following God made relationships and intimacy more difficult. If the goal was connection, the church created a lose/lose scenario. If you failed at living perfectly, you felt alone or worse, if you succeeded, like me, you felt even more alone.

In SA, lawyers showed up in their BMWs and homeless people arrived on the bus. No one there cared about my financial competency. At SA, everyone was treated the same because victory wasn't seen as an individual accomplishment. Members believed that in order to remove something as powerful as shame it must be a community endeavor. SA didn't see the primary problem as not having enough information, expertise, or morality. They saw the fundamental problem as a lack of connection — something that takes an entire community to correct. Every week we read:

> *"Many of us felt inadequate, unworthy, alone, and afraid. Our insides never matched what we saw on the outsides of others. Early on, we came to feel disconnected--from parents, from peers, from ourselves."*

This was me, but not from before I had met Jesus, like I had told in my story. This was me now.

In SA, while it didn't feel like we were becoming experts in anything, or getting more qualified, or becoming respectable…I felt something new, something Jesus had never helped me with.

For that hour that I listened to people share… I didn't feel alone.

I felt connected.

The Cost Of Intimacy

You would think that listening to a bunch of grown men (there were also a few women) talk about how they had masturbated, looked at porn, and failed in their marriages would be depressing. But it wasn't. Something about the fact that they showed up to the meeting and said, "I'm not where I want to be, but I haven't given up yet" created hope. It told me that when failure happened, the same shame that brought isolation could also be used to create connection.

Going to 10 a.m. church services in the sanctuary after the 7 a.m. basement meetings started to feel a little silly. After hearing the broad range of a weekly experience that involved heartbreak, tears, graphic details and the emotional high that comes with seeing your friends survive another week, it felt shallow to sit next to a bunch of people I hardly knew and repeat words like "I'm filled with joy because Jesus died for me" or "no one's perfect." These phrases now felt shallow and impotent. We all looked good but I knew what was behind the curtain and I couldn't ignore it anymore. At church it felt like we were there to maintain appearances, not actually get help. Our priority was to increase our moral standing in our community and with each other — a goal that, when accomplished, only made me more miserable.

In SA, members had given up their moral standing. Simply walking through the door meant admitting moral bankruptcy and a need for help. Every week members gave up their sleep and sat in shitty metal folding chairs drinking the shitty coffee to connect with me.

But the most important thing they gave up, the thing that went beyond any price tag and the thing that I had been unable to find any place else was people willing to give up their dignity. Being in SA meant losing respect or even your job if the public found out. But in the face of these consequences, members had decided it was worth it.

At SA I felt like I was in a war. A war against evil or myself, I'm not really sure which, but one thing was clear every single week: I was not in this war alone. And this feeling of not being alone, this connection, is what people in SA wanted. And for this connection to happen, it became clear to me that these very failures I had kept hidden were the ticket to forging the strongest bonds.

Members frequently told stories about calling others when they were at their lowest and shared how companionship in their darkest moments altered their behavior, saved their marriage, or even literally their lives. We needed each other. For the first time in my life I was necessary, not as an inspiration on a pedestal but as an ally in the trenches.

Until now, I had maintained my status in SA as an observer. I was distant. I respected the members but I didn't consider myself one. I still maintained plausible deniability. But if I was going to ever experience this same connection that I was seeing around me, I needed to have the same attitude I had with Christianity. I needed to go all-in.

<u>My Sponsor</u>

In SA they say to:

    1. Go to meetings.

    2. Get a sponsor.

Even though I didn't want more commitments, I wanted to succeed, whatever that meant. Plus, I couldn't ignore the results that these actions were having on those around me. I decided to commit further. Some people went to meetings every day which seemed excessive. One a week was fine for me. But I needed a sponsor. I went to the guy everyone talked about the most. His name was William and he had been sober for 20 years. Submission had always worked for me in the past. If I wanted the fastest growth, I knew this was the way to get it. In SA, I decided to submit to William.

We met at the coffee shop in Whole Foods. William was a bus driver and always wore brown dress pants with a freshly pressed, collared shirt, unless he was on break from work. Then it was a navy blue shirt with a *King County Metro* logo embroidered on his chest. He had thin gray hair that was always dyed a shade too orange so that it never looked quite natural. At our first meeting, William asked me about my week. I knew the details that sponsors expected from this type of question and it felt dangerous to open up. I thought "this sicko probably gets off on hearing details about how guys whack off or what kind of porn they view." I stared blankly. "I don't know where to start," I said.

"Talk about the thing you least want to talk about," he said. There was a five minute pause.

Another five minutes passed as I slowly sipped my coffee while William crunched his salad. William meticulously cut up and packed his salads at home and never used dressing.

I took a deep breath. "Kami and I got in a fight last night and I looked at porn." I had conflicting expectations. On the one hand I was waiting for the shaming look and then condescending advice that was normal in church. On the other hand, I knew this guy had been airing his dirty laundry for 20 years. A simple fight and some porn wouldn't be that interesting.

But William's reaction shocked me. By his look you would have assumed I had just given him the goddamn hidden map to Atlantis. His face lit up. "Oh, wonderful. Thank you SO much for sharing."

William wasn't interested in details. He had heard them all. Years later I would have no problem sharing mine on the most public platforms that existed but for now it felt like each detail could kill me. What William understood is that the details aren't as important as the shame they represent.

Some people felt shame over the type of porn they looked at, some felt it about the shape of their body, and some felt it about not living up to the standard set by their religious community. Regardless of the behavior, William was obsessed with seeing all forms of shame disappear.

Shame creates isolation. In SA, if connection is the solution, then shame is the enemy. William knew there was only one cure for shame: you speak it out loud. Or in spiritual language, you confess it. Unlike church, it wasn't good enough to say you had confessed it to God in your private prayer time. No, you had to confess it to another human. The secret to beating isolation was to share.

Boot Camp

So, just like I had done in the church, I submitted. I wanted to figure out how I could get the secret sauce from SA in my own life. And sure enough, submitting to a sponsor worked. Where before I was left to try and observe patterns and translate them myself, now I had a person dedicated to prying out parts of me I didn't even know existed. William had all these tips and tricks to unearth things inside my darkest corners. It was like Sherlock Holmes combined with Howard Stern and became my shrink.

He started me off simply. I was talking about how difficult it was to parent, especially a boy. My boy would scream and throw a temper tantrum and I thought I was doing pretty well walking away instead of spanking him till I saw blood. But this didn't impress William.

"Hold him," he said.

"What?" I asked.

"Hold him," he said.

"How long?" I asked.

"Until he's done crying," he said.

"Sometimes he screams for an hour," I said.

"Hold him," he said. And I did. At first it was the most painful and awkward thing I had ever experienced. But through William, I could see that our method of distancing ourselves wasn't helping our kids. I was just afraid of them.

The part of me that was not held as a little boy did not think it was ok for little boys to cry. When it started, I needed it to stop. There were two ways. Silence the child which got violent, or create distance. In church, they didn't seem to care how your children got well-behaved, only that they were. William wasn't concerned with behavior or appearances. His method led me to new depths of compassion for my son and myself.

Most of the things William said to me sounded crazy at first. But the more I let it sit, and eventually obey, his crazy ideas became life-changing. William told me to go to three meetings a week. By now I had moved to Kentucky for work and to be closer to my mentor, business partner, and in-law Jeremiah. There was only one meeting a week here. "Start meetings," he said. So I did, at the only available time which was 6 a.m.

William had even crazier ideas. He put me through 90 days and then 180 days of abstinence so I could see what was behind my sex drive. Something I never would have imagined. The idea seemed painful to me. I brought it up to Kami and was surprised to find out Kami was afraid, too. Kami and I had a pretty limited vocabulary when it came to feelings, attachment styles, and trauma and sex was often the only way we knew to communicate and feel connected.

Our Christian friends thought we were crazy for even considering this. In the end, I decided if SA was real, I would need to go all-in to see if it could help me. Kami agreed and these periods of abstinence brought us help, freedom and a changed relationship. I often walked away after implementing one of William's "suggestions" with more information than I would have gained from a college course and more strength than I would have gained in a military boot camp. SA was working. I was changing.

Behind The Behavior

They have a saying in SA — "It's never about the sex." Sex is just the symptom. SA taught that people who don't know how to process difficult emotions like rejection, confusion, and fear, use sex to medicate their pain.

In church, we focused all of our attention on behaviors and didn't care what caused them. To us, it was always as simple as "sin." But in SA, I learned that a wide range of addictive behaviors like alcohol, shopping, or drugs could all be used to mask pain. I used Bible studies to mask mine.

Focusing on different behaviors had made it difficult for me to relate to other SA members. They seemed damaged. I always thought my childhood was great. We went to Disneyland and my parents introduced me to Jesus. What more could a kid ask for? To establish my success, I focused on more behaviors. I was a faithful husband (aka not divorced), a non-drug user, and didn't use swear words. I defined my success based upon verses cherry-picked from the Bible. And these very limited successes made me ignore most any pain or other failures, writing them off as "no big deal," simply because they did not fit into my narrative.

One day, when I was wrestling with one member's particularly horrid actions (William visited this member in prison), I was shocked when, after hearing his backstory from William, I was even able to sympathize with this monster. William said that if I was raised the same way others were, into their family system, with their parents, I would be just like them. For the first time I could see that I was just like the other people in the room, even though they weren't Christians. We believed different things, but it didn't matter.

When I started to be less judgmental toward others, I started to be less judgmental about myself. Certain parts of my psyche had been suppressed and hidden since I had accepted Jesus into my heart because they didn't line up with who I was *supposed* to be. I had always blamed myself for my behaviors. The blame had prevented me from being able to talk about myself objectively. I was much harsher on myself than I was on other people. The people in the basement said that the things that happened to me weren't my fault. They believed that these events, whether we remembered them or not, held power over us and the way we released that power was by talking about them.

Now I started to face my pain for the first time. A flood of memories came back of things I had blocked. Some of these things were things that had happened to me like being spanked. Some were things I had done to other people. For the first time in a decade, I remembered the $12,000 I had stolen from my friends.

Now, instead of memorizing Bible verses, I spent my mental energy asking a new set of questions: What did my family system teach me? Did I have trauma? Was there a deeper reason I did the things I did? I wondered what patterns triggered stress in my own life and why I felt inadequate. I didn't have answers to these questions but just the questions brought me comfort. While I had always believed that "the good news" and heaven were the most important things in my life, they now started to feel a little shallow. Those concepts hadn't saved the parts of myself that I was hiding. They hadn't saved the parts that other Christians were hiding. In fact, they seemed to make it worse. But now I had discovered a new order in the universe.

Salvation 2.0

I came to SA as an observer and the highest goal I could imagine was escaping guilt by ending masturbation and porn. But eventually I saw other parts of my life change that went far beyond those goals. Attending meetings and obeying William's suggestions was starting to work its magic.

One day I was walking through Costco and saw the movie *Speed Racer* on the big flat-screen TVs. There was a cheesy scene where the main character wins the race at the end and it shows the dad's face that is so proud — he was played by John Goodman. I just started crying and I had no idea why. I hadn't cried in ten years. I had shut off so many impulses as a child that many other connected sensitivities and functions I didn't even know existed had shut down, as well. It turns out you don't get to choose to just shut down a few isolated and undesired habits. Anesthesia numbs it all. I just thought that some activities, like dancing and crying, were for other people, not me. Now, systems I didn't know existed were coming back online. Crying started to happen more, not just when I was sad but at the end of kids' movies like *Speed Racer* and *Ratatouille*.

I had always seen salvation as something that happened *after* we died. I had spent my entire life telling people about it but never experienced it myself. But now, I started to see that my fixation on heaven was less about faith and more about denial. I started to feel like what was happening to me because of SA and William was salvation. Piece by piece, habit by habit, parts of me that were lost, banished, and cut off, were being saved, welcomed back, and restored.

I had always dreamed of helping people as an author but had never been able to do it by preaching down to people. But the perspective I was discovering in the basement felt more life-changing than accepting Jesus into my heart. I wondered if there was a way to take this message to the world so it could help others. This seemed impossible because I hadn't even been able to share anything or help anyone in SA. How could I speak up anywhere else if I couldn't even say a word in the safety of the basement?

Put Your Oxygen Mask On First

I didn't want to like the people in the basement. But I couldn't help it. Gradually, I started to feel more invested in Bob, who had cheated on his wife, or Steve, who had exposed himself to school kids, or Gina, who hopped from one relationship to another, than the people up in church. I hated to admit it, but these people were becoming my friends. I felt like I knew and cared about them more than I did impressing the people at church who only saw my best. But my relationships in SA were one-sided. I was taking but not giving. I didn't mind sharing with William, but sharing my secrets in front of the group felt crippling. I knew I couldn't impress them, but even though they were nobodies, I couldn't stand looking foolish. The longer I went, the more I felt like a fraud, just like I had back at church.

One day my sponsor, William, asked me why I hadn't shared yet.

"I don't know what to say," I said. "It sounds like everyone knows more than I do and I have nothing new to add."

"You don't understand the purpose of the shares," he said. "You don't share for others, you share for yourself. You say the thing you need to say."

"That sounds selfish."

My whole life I was trained to ignore my own desires and needs and put others before myself. I wanted to love and help others – to offer them direction, inspiration, answers, and truth. Now I could see that my belief in love was a crutch keeping me from *actually* loving people.

"The best thing you can do for others…. is to put your own oxygen mask on first."

Sharing is for you. The fact that others benefit is a side effect.

Saving My Ass

Even though my experience in SA was life-changing, I kept my involvement a secret from anyone in the outside world. If people at church or Bible camp found out, my reputation would be shot. The same fear of being found out that had kept me hidden for most of my life now kept me silent in the basement.

I had spent the first 30 years of my life building and protecting a reputation. A good, strong and false reputation. I presented the edited version of what I thought was acceptable and helpful and I was good at it. But sponsors have a way of putting things simply and bluntly.

One day at coffee William said, "Ben, you can save your ass, or you can save your face."

The emphasis was on the word "*or.*" William had seen hundreds of people go through the program and he knew you couldn't choose both. If you truly want healing and growth in the deepest way, you have to be able to sacrifice your reputation to get it.

I was coming up on my one year anniversary of attending SA. I still maintained my observer status and only listened, not saying a word in meetings. I related to others, and saw my struggles in theirs, yet still distanced myself in the ways that mattered the most. I was browsing but not committing. I wanted to be able to relate to sexaholics but saw myself as superior.

But this is not the way SA members had found success. While membership in this club was simple, it was not easy. The most common phrase was "half measures availed us nothing." Every SA member knew you couldn't be halfway. It's like being half a virgin. Better to be all-in.

Save my ass or save my face?

William showed me it was one or the other.

Membership

I loved being an observer in the basement. I loved the vibe, the way it made me understand and embrace my past, and the way it helped me express compassion to those whose behavior was on the fringe of society, something Christianity was never able to help me with. The only thing I wasn't willing to do was to become a member myself by claiming the title of sexaholic.

I had made excuses about the label and its accuracy. I was "just as bad as a sexaholic," I said, adopting a quasi-member status. Just like I always had done, I hid behind vagueness. I had never had sex with anyone else or cheated on Kami. By now, I could see that most people looked at porn. The only difference was that I admitted it. Should this make me a sexaholic? By my math, I should be less of a sexaholic than others. Why should I take the title?

Each of these technicalities resulted in me focusing on how different I was from those in the basement. And yet all of the stories, the meetings, the conversations with William and even the way I had read the Bible was bringing me to the same conclusion: I was the same as these people who were all claiming that they were sexaholics. This group of people was the best chance I had of fitting in and being accepted, anywhere. These people were my friends. While neither Bob, Steve nor Gina impressed me, they made me feel less alone.

So, while William phrased it as a choice between saving my ass or saving my face, I saw it as a choice to choose connection from the only people who were offering it. Or choose another 20 years of loneliness.

There was no 30-day trial. If I accepted the title of sex addict, there would be no turning back. In the vernacular, there were no ex-sex addicts. Calling myself a sex addict would be the funeral of my ego and reputation — something I had sacrificed my summers for, spent my life building, and defined the entire world by. But the other way had cost me any true intimacy and I was no longer willing to pay that price. Given the choice between respect and connection, I wanted connection.

The next week, I walked into the dingy basement and sat down in a metal folding chair. I had studied this room for two years but somehow had never been a part of it. I could save my ass or I could save my face. I had spent my first three decades saving my face. I didn't know what it meant but it was time to save my ass. I didn't tell Kami my plans, but I knew she would support me.

When the sharing time opened, I was the first person to speak. "I'm Ben, I'm a sexaholic."

4: The Cost
Sharing's Price

__Acceptance__

My first share in the basement I didn't say much. Just something about how hard it had been for me to share and how growing up in the church I never felt like I fit in. But I committed to my act of courage. Now I felt exposed and wanted to scurry away as fast as possible.

The group wouldn't have it. Just like when I had become baptized into the church, the witnesses were ready to throw a party. But, unlike the church, these people weren't celebrating my affirmation of a code of beliefs, they were celebrating my courage to share. Instantly a line formed. Gina said, "Thanks for your share. I feel the same way. Can I give you a hug?" Steve said, "I've been there, it feels good not to be alone." And Bob said, "I grew up in the church, too. I've felt a similar thing but never knew how to put it into words."

This feedback was like a shot of adrenaline. Even though I technically knew I would be accepted, telling my story, hearing the affirmation and feeling the presence of those surrounding me afterward, was tangible. Unlike my baptism, where membership felt shaky and conditional on good behavior and well-maintained secrets, Sexaholics Anonymous accepted me at my worst. I was in. So what next?

William had been telling me about another process in SA and now that I was a member, I was ready to start. I created a sexual inventory of every sexual event from my life that I had felt shame around and "gave it away" by reading it to the group. My inventory ranged from the first time I saw a lady in her underwear in a dressing room to my most recent pattern with Kami of withdrawal, porn and masturbation. This process took two years of writing, remembering, procrastinating, and writing some more. The final draft was seven pages.

I read my inventory in a Sunday morning meeting in the basement and the line to talk to me took 45 minutes to get through as people thanked me for sharing a story that helped them to process their own and feel understood. I had been more vulnerable than I ever had in my life.

Unlike my church community, my SA friends weren't just people who begrudgingly accepted my worst moments. Hearing about my worst moments was key to their escape from shame. In this group, I felt like I could be myself for the first time. I felt a calm peace I had never felt before. My shoulders relaxed for the first time in my adult life. There was a group of people I had no fear of being found out with. It felt so good. This is what it meant to put my oxygen mask on first. There was nothing I could do to scare them away. I would soon find out, the same was not true of the outside world.

Going Public

Now that I was a full-fledged member I decided to come out of the closet and risk inviting some of my church friends to SA. After all, many of them had been open with me by admitting that they "struggled with lust" and continually "dropped the ball" and I thought some of them could find help in the vulnerable sharing I had witnessed in meetings.

Most thought I was crazy. A few considered it and two came. "Wow, that's a lot to take in, but I don't think it's for me," one said. Neither came back.

My Sunday schedule was to go to the 7 a.m. meeting, go home, have breakfast with the family, and then head to church at 10 a.m.. People, both at church and the Bible camp, sensed a radical fearlessness that had always been in my life but was now combined with self-acceptance and uninhibited storytelling. People didn't understand it but admired me more than ever.

I just saw what I was learning in SA as an extension of the Christian message that I had heard Jesus talk about since I was a child. To me, it felt impossible to restrict what I had learned in SA to the basement the same way I didn't restrict what I heard in church to Sunday mornings. If these things were true, it seemed like they should affect every area of our lives, especially our homes.

Our businesses were wildly successful. I had taken my knowledge of running a blackjack team to building the largest blackjack training website on the internet with my best friend. Together, we would fly down to Vegas and train people how to play blackjack, getting paid $30,000 for a weekend. With my video advertising startup, I had two income streams and more money than I knew what to do with.

With our family in Kentucky, just across the river from downtown Cincinnati, I started buying up the houses on our block and filling them with friends. A friend from Bible college moved across the country, and the COO of our video startup moved two doors down with his family. Another young couple asked if Kami and I would mentor them and soon moved into our attic. We celebrated religious meals every week, studied the Bible twice a week with the kids, shared homeschooling duties, went on intentional retreats and vacations and were at each other's births. We had a full-blown commune that would combine my desire to follow Jesus with the radical practices of intimacy I was learning in SA. Life was perfect.

Or so I thought.

<u>Disqualified</u>

My mentor, business partner, and in-law Jeremiah's influence had grown, too. Although he still sported the t-shirt with flannel wrapped around his waist, he had graduated from khaki cargo pants to blue jeans as his full-time uniform. He had a community a few miles away that we modeled ours after and got training from. I continued to model my life after his and seek his guidance on how to apply our Christian faith to business and family. He was the most respected Christian leader in the area, being sought out by mega churches to speak and lead classes on family and following Jesus.

While my community had benefited from my work in SA, I had limited my conversations to a few close friends, being careful to stick to the Christian vocabulary when talking to groups or posting publicly. I kept certain stories hidden from my Christian friends but this took a ton of energy and I was no longer sure who I was protecting: them or me? I didn't want to maintain a split personality and decided to come out in the grandest way I knew how, on my blog — the place I had used for preaching the message of Jesus and dishing out Christian advice. Like I had always done before big decisions, I went to Jeremiah with my plan and, just like after our birth, he had a warning:

"People will not understand. You will be disqualifying yourself from ministry for no reason. You've worked so hard and now you will be throwing away everyone's trust. People do not need to see all your dirty laundry. There are better ways to help those you care about. Take some time and think about it."

He said the things I had spent my whole life believing. He wanted me to keep the parts of myself hidden that I had spent my whole life covering up. But he hadn't seen what I had seen in SA and I just wanted so badly for my church family to accept who I really was. Like he suggested, I took some time to think about it, but in the end, I was ready to move forward. I not-so-subtly titled the post: "I'm Ben and I'm a sexaholic."

The response was swift. My wife and I had applied to volunteer at the Bible camp that summer for a month. The place we met, where we had always been welcomed; our home away from home. "In light of your recent confession, we think you'll understand why we can't allow you to be around the youth as you present a threat to their safety and well-being," the letter read. It finished with, "We will pray for you and hope you can find healing from your sin."

I was surprised. I shouldn't have been but I was. The word "sexaholic" was the most common phrase spoken in the basement. It brought intimacy and healing. But spoken in the outside world, the same word brought a reputational death sentence. In my experience, those in SA who talked about their struggles were far less of a threat than those inside the church who bottled them up. In SA, I didn't become more of a sex addict. I had gotten healthier, more honest, more humble, and more connected to God — the things we had talked about in church for years. I had never cheated on my wife, molested any kids, or violated anyone's boundaries. It wasn't actual danger the church was afraid of, it was the appearance of it. The only difference between me and those at church wasn't that I had struggles, it was that I was talking about them, and now I was penalized for it and labeled unsafe.

But beyond the safety of the kids, there was another reason my new status was threatening to them and that had to do with the safety of the institution. The church claimed to have the answers for all of life and didn't play well with others. It would be like if the spokesperson for Weight Watchers was also going to Jenny Craig. The definition of *Christian, forgiven and loved by God*, was supposed to be the only title I needed. It freed me from bad behavior and the need for all other lesser forms of help. By even considering dual membership, I was admitting that the solutions in the church weren't working for me. I was off script.

The backbone of the church was preaching. To preach well you had to pretend that you lived exactly what you preached, even if you didn't. So for them, sharing, even if it was honest, wasn't seen as a step forward, it was seen as a step backward.

Getting rejected by camp and hearing "I told you so" by my mentor had the reverse effect of what one might expect. Instead of becoming more timid, I felt the opposite. In the church, we had always talked about unconditional love and acceptance of both God and His followers. Now the love and acceptance started to feel very conditional and I wanted to explore the boundaries.

The Vlog

The boldness I had tested in coming out as a sexaholic was starting to spread to other areas of my life. I had fantasized about being an author since high school. I had also dreamed of making videos that communicated complex messages that I cared about, not just the advertisements I made for tech giants. Excuse after excuse backlogged me and the notebooks of ideas still sat on my shelf accumulating dust. But now I could feel urgency welling and there was less and less holding me back.

I had a deep fear of pride in presenting my own ideas. The only way I could conceive of a YouTube channel was to make videos like my friend John was doing — explaining someone else's ideas. I was so scared of making content that featured myself that I had plans to make stick figure puppets that summarized every chapter of the french classic Les Miserables. The 365 chapters of the book would have taken me two years if I did five videos a week!

But, because of SA, I was starting to see power in telling my own story. Unlike church, where we only told God's story, in SA the majority of the meetings were spent just sharing about one's own story. Hearing these stories is what had helped members so much. I wondered if sharing my story outside of SA could help others the same way. That's when I discovered a new video format: vlogging. Vlogs were a consistent series of video diaries that had fun clips of cats and catchy music mixed in. "We have cats," I thought.

The timing of my new idea felt perfect. I had a weekly phone call with my friend and old business partner, John, the one who had built the YouTube channel explaining the Bible. His channel was a wild success, had a staff of dozens, and had just passed a million subscribers. He had offered to help me, so I told him my idea of starting a vlog. "Why are you making these videos? Don't you think this is just a way to draw attention to yourself and build a following? The Christian life is not about getting more followers. I'm happy to help you in coming up with another idea." I was devastated. I had been friends with John for 20 years. I knew I couldn't do this alone. I didn't know anything about YouTube and I needed support. So I went to the only place I knew I would have it: Kami. "This is not going to make any money. It will take eight hours a day. For it to work, it's gonna take over our whole life and I'm gonna need you to be a part of it so when I ask you to talk about stuff on camera, I'm gonna need you to trust me." It was a big ask.

Kami was conservative and private by nature. She was introverted and it took a lot of energy for her to share. While I enjoyed crafting messages and didn't mind being on stage, Kami didn't like public speaking.

Kami had seen me come alive as parts of me were unlocked. She didn't know how it was all going to work out. After all, strategy was not really Kami's thing. But loyalty was. Even though she didn't have any ideas for the videos, and she didn't know how to edit, and she didn't know how YouTube worked, she knew me. Now, she looked me in the eye. "I can tell this is important to you. You NEED to do it. I trust you and I will support you, whatever it takes."

Sharing my life on a public platform was scary and I knew I would face scrutiny from my church friends. My Christian friends saw my membership in SA as threatening and now I had found a larger platform to share my story. I began to fear more repercussions. If I was going to stand a chance at vlogging, I needed accountability. I needed an authority to submit to. In the Christian world I submitted to my mentor. In SA I submitted to my sponsor. For my vlog, I didn't have a boss. So I made one. I would submit to a schedule. Monday, Wednesday, and Friday I would publish a video. My first one went out on September 28, 2015. Publishing vlogs was much harder than I thought but I edited and published each video no matter how much I hated it. I had to learn everything from scratch and didn't see any benefit. I just knew I wouldn't be able to live with myself if I quit. I adopted a mentality I had used in Christianity which was to act as if my life depended on it. This was something I once thought was saving me from a literal hell of burning fire but now I felt like it was saving me from a different kind of hell, one represented by stacks and stacks of journals that illustrated my fractured self, unfulfilled destiny, and lack of courage.

Document

While I had started sharing more in the basement, I didn't know how to translate honest sharing into my regular life or writing. In SA, they celebrated honesty by saying "thanks for sharing" when you were finished. In the real world, my honesty was penalized and got me banned from camp. And so I looked at what was being done on YouTube and just copied the most popular vloggers. This meant our vlog consisted of highly edited "best of" moments of our day. The videos were polished and designed to show people how important kids were, inspire others by showing them the highlights of our marriage and encourage people to think of their family outside the box. They often featured ten minutes of me talking, sharing my ideas and offering my help. While my editing was improving, our videos were having the same impact as the Christian t-shirts I wore in high school: none. They were still just another, more subtle form of preaching. My audience, about 30 people, was bored, stagnant, and irritated. In addition to that, I didn't want the distraction of money so I completely demonetized my channel. This meant I wasn't changing anyone's mind, making any money, and my videos sucked.

I reverted to preaching when it came to displaying our family on YouTube because it was safe. But I thought about my time in SA. Week after week I heard people entertain, inspire, and captivate with their vulnerability and honesty. In SA I had learned that the truth is enough. You don't have to refer to a code of beliefs and you don't need to make shit up. And so I started to reconsider what honesty and courage in sharing could look like for our vlog. The secret to sharing came when I heard social media superstar Gary Vee give a teenager advice: "Stop telling people what to do, just turn on your camera and document your life." But what was there for me to document?

Lead With Your Weakness

In SA, I saw that the best way to make a connection is by sharing failures, not successes. My sponsor, William, was clearly the most respected guy in the room. He was a leader but he never played the part of an expert. He never gave advice and he constantly shared in grisly detail how he had fumbled that week. At first it was confusing because I thought the longer you were in SA, the stronger and less reproachable you would become. But the opposite was true with William. He seemed to fail more than others. At first this was discouraging. But then I could see that it wasn't that William was failing more, it was just that he was the most honest person in the room. Sharing his secret of leadership one day at the coffee shop in Whole Foods he said, "Ben, you're used to leading with your strength. To succeed in SA, you lead with your weakness."

At church, we celebrated Jesus' weakness but we always led with our strength. This is why it had been so scary for me to share. William believed vulnerability was the truest form of strength. All my life I had focused on how polish, expertise and knowledge could serve as a beacon of hope toward others — all examples of strength that elevated me above my audience.

The same was true for my vlogs and writing. My goal was always to display virtue and inspire others. Heroes were shiny and strong and always won out over temptation. This was the type of hero I wanted to be and how I presented myself. Since the age of four I had only presented what I thought I should be, not who I actually was. But this presentation made me flat and unrelatable. For the first time I understood that my problem in communication wasn't with my audience — something completely outside of my control. My audience wanted vulnerable sharing. They wanted connection and my writing had never offered it. In church I learned people admire perfection. In SA I learned that they relate to failure. You don't win an audience over with virtue. You win them over with vulnerability. You don't create comrades by leading with your strength. You get them by leading with your weakness.

I saw the world in a certain way but I tried to convince myself that I didn't because I shouldn't. Now that the shouldn't was gone I could finally be honest. I could finally share myself and I could finally allow people to appreciate me and appreciate the way I saw the world.

I had always spent my life hiding my weaknesses in my family. But now I started to look at what actually happened in a normal week at our house. What could I document if I wasn't worried about hiding? This is what I found:

1. **Fights with Kami**. Kami and I had a cycle where I would withdraw from her. I was unresponsive and did not initiate conversations or touch. Instead of our norm of sleeping naked, we would wear clothes to bed and I would avoid her at all costs. During these times, I would go into depressive slumps and my productivity and social activity would halt. Kami would accuse me of trying to punish her. I felt extreme guilt but had no idea how to stop the cycle. I felt embarrassed and didn't know how to get help.

2. **Unorthodox life**. As much as I had tried to fit in, it was never natural for me. Our house looked like it was decorated by merging a farm, a schoolhouse, and a hippie commune. We smoked cigars, ran marathons, and didn't wear bike helmets or have health insurance. Our schedule had the intentionality of an army boot camp but swung wildly from having no rules for our kids for an entire year to training rigorously for ultra marathons.

3. **Frustration and failure as a parent**. We had talked about children being a blessing and how wonderful they were. But deep down I struggled with acceptance, rejection, confidence and anger. We were confused about how to parent when it came to sex, drugs, and screen time and I felt like most of our parenting methods were driving our kids away.

I had never mentioned these parts publicly but these were the things I spent the most time and energy on internally. Slowly but surely I started to embrace these parts of myself. Seeing this new side of myself was like getting eyesight for the first time. The very things I wanted to protect, my weakness, were some of the best things I could share with my audience.

The first time we were in the middle of a fight and turned on the camera we didn't know what to say. So, I started just like the first time I shared in SA by saying, "I don't know what to say." Kami looked scared and depressed. And then we started talking. We each shared our feelings; the pain, the confusion, nothing tied up in a little bow, just messy, like it felt.

When we published the video, people took sides. They made judgments saying I was too controlling or Kami seemed dead and distant. People were used to us being inspirational, even if it was false. But instead of spending my energy trying to defend ourselves, I spent my energy asking if the videos were accurate and if they led with our weakness. Instead of posturing our relationship to look successful from a pedestal, we invited viewers into our experience and let them be frustrated with us.

Oversharing

When I started sharing things I had spent my whole life hiding, I had no idea where the line was for privacy, cringe, or helpfulness. Reading my sexual inventory in the basement, the wild feeling of acceptance was so refreshing after decades of a double life. I was so afraid of going back to the shame and secrets that I started sharing my inventory without discretion to anyone who would listen. First my wife, then my siblings, then our parents. Reading it to my in-laws was the most awkward as they sat in their matching Polo Ralph Lauren outfits. Jeremiah's wife, who wore unfitted Bible Belt mom jeans with a floral blouse, fidgeted the whole time. At the end she just stared and looked down awkwardly and shuffled her feet. "Wow, I had no idea," she said. No one knew what to do with these stories. Unlike SA, there were no thank-yous or words of how they could relate.

Online, our oversharing was just as bad. We were sloppy. We started oversharing about our sex problems. The details painted a picture people did not want to see. I shared about how I had gotten angry with my kid and wanted to throw him across the room. We talked about our fights. I talked about how I had looked at porn. I talked about how I had been disappointed when my wife said she wasn't interested in having sex and how we had created a schedule for sex as a compromise. Critics called us obsessed and friends who had supported us tuned out. I was the epitome of TMI. Eventually I read my entire sexual inventory on our YouTube channel. More than 4,000 people tuned in to hear every detail of my weird, repressed, and perverted history.

Because my honesty had helped me so much in the basement, I thought it was my duty to be transparent with everyone. I had no filter for who my sharing was beneficial for or if it would help or hurt me. We weren't publishing for our audience. We were publishing for ourselves. I had felt trapped by my shadow side for so long that many things I said were just because I needed to hear them said out loud. I was so afraid of going back to the double life that had isolated me that I was willing to scare people away, burn bridges, and lose our audience to be compulsively honest.

My Worst Fear

My boldness and lack of filter for keeping secrets spread to every topic and platform. So, when the largest radio show in the world, NPR's This American Life asked to interview me about blackjack, I agreed. And when they asked me a question about honesty and large sums of cash, I answered by telling the story of how I had lied to my friends about the $12,000. It helped that my process in SA had led me to going back and apologizing to my friends and paying them back the money I had stolen. My friends were understanding. Would the business clients I had, like Google or Facebook, be so understanding? How would they feel knowing that the person they had chosen to run their project, share their message and build trust with their audience had stolen five figures from his best friends?

My mentor Jeremiah's words before I wrote the blog post about being a sexaholic came to mind:

"People will not understand. You've worked so hard and now you will be throwing away everyone's trust. People do not need to see all your dirty laundry. Take some time and think about it."

Who was I really benefiting here? Did the world *really* need to hear the most embarrassing moment of my adult life?

Kami and I sat close in the kitchen, huddled over the radio as the story was broadcast to the entire world. It was too late now. I would never be able to land a business deal again. I would never be trusted by a friend or be in spiritual leadership. My authority as an author was compromised. Who would buy a book written by a thief?

Kami looked at me while holding my hand and said, "I'm proud of you." And then we waited for the world to respond.

What happened next?

Nothing.

No one called me to cancel their friendship. No clients asked for their money back. Unlike the church, the outside world seemed more forgiving. A few people texted me and said "I heard your story on NPR. You've finally made it." It was like they missed the part about me stealing. The most terrifying part of my entire life was boring to others. No one even cared.

It was like the universe looked at me and said, "Is that all you got? *Yawn.*"

No One Cares About Your Ego

I was surprised to discover that no one in the outside world cared about my moral success. Protecting my reputation was dramatic for me because my ego didn't want to die.

But my ego does not exist to others. The drama I feared wasn't real. It was manufactured in a game that I had invented.

When I was on this American Life, my friends viewed me as a hero. No one even blinked at my confession. In fact, the year my secret came out was the same year I was voted Ernst & Young Entrepreneur of the Year — the most prestigious business award in the city, proving that my fear was not based in reality.

Invincible

I wasn't aware of how much energy I was spending to protect my secrets until I no longer had any. There was a veil of secrecy around every relationship, topic, or activity that I thought could ruin me. Now that I was free from this shame, I was able to see who I was and what I cared about in a way I was unable to access when the voices protecting my ego were the loudest.

By sitting back, fearing that I would constantly be exposed, I had handed control of my life over to a universal and invisible enemy that would never go away. My strategy of protecting secrets prevented intimacy and freedom. By exposing myself, sure I had offended some and confused others, but I had also kicked shame in the balls, took control of my life and stopped living in fear. I had shared the most incriminating details of the most shameful things I had ever done and now these secrets that had defined me no longer held any power. By publicly trash talking myself in the worst way, I had faced my fears and won. Now I had nothing to lose. I felt invincible.

No More Holy Rolling

I had always focused my art toward impressing the moral elite. I needed connection and I was willing to give up myself to get it. But the moral elite always preferred the isolation and illusion of holiness over connection. This is why no one from our old life was interested in hearing about our new perspective. After a lot of wasted effort, I concluded that trying to change people's minds who were committed to not changing was a waste of time. They didn't deserve my loyalty or effort. I didn't have the power to change the church. It would go on. I just couldn't be a part of it.

I always positioned myself so the moral elite would listen and by offering them my honesty and energy I had nothing to give to the outcasts, the black sheep of the world, the misfits. This was the group that I had always felt more attracted to, the group that felt like me. If I was going to connect with other outcasts, I needed to try something new. Some changes I made were subtle. We started to swear in our videos. Our whole lives we had not been allowed to say these words, and now instead of censoring ourselves or editing it out, we just talked the way we normally talked to each other.

We got feedback instantly from our Christian audience. "What's the deal with the cussing? The language seems completely unnecessary!" They were still operating as if the purpose of my art was to promote their moral code. We got similar reactions when we started sharing our true feelings and frustrations in our marriage. The moral elite said it was TMI and cringy.

But now I could see the problem wasn't with me, it was with my audience. There was a new audience out there, I just had never seen them. But, with my art I would find them.

A Threat

Even though our vlogs were still only getting 30 views each, the brutal honesty and candidness of our videos had resulted in an audience that started to trust us. These videos were having the opposite effect on my church friends.

My church friends said they valued freedom and honesty. They also told us that they "loved and supported and were praying for me" but no one asked any questions about my videos or ever acknowledged that they were watching them.

Instead, I got questions like "How does Kami feel about you sharing everything so publicly online?" And "Who are you submitting to now?"

Even though we talked about the value of confession a lot in church, nothing like this existed between those four walls. The way I was sharing broke the image that they were trying to maintain of what a successful Christian looked like — an image my friends were still trying to keep up. Back in the men's group, when we confessed around the round table about "dropping the ball", there was a sense of groveling and the need for the tribe's endorsement and approval. This was expressed as those around the table reaffirmed the truths of Scripture, cementing their importance in the ongoing powerlessness and dependence of the individual. But I didn't feel powerless anymore. I felt more powerful than ever. Because of SA, my confessions no longer carried shame and I wasn't apologizing or asking for help from anyone at church. I wasn't groveling, I was no longer asking anyone's permission, and I was doing it on the largest platform in the world.

I thought I was following God's Word and acting more like Jesus by being more honest and transparent. But, as a respected leader, my sharing was seen as disruptive and as a threatening bid for power. The leaders in the church saw me as dangerous.

A Week Off

Two months after starting the vlog, Jeremiah came to me. He had had enough. He didn't mention the vlog but he said he was concerned I had a problem with pride. "You've changed. Things have gotten worse." The word *narcissist* was mentioned.

"Our work is supposed to bring glory to God, not just bring attention to ourselves," he said. "Are you still willing to submit to me as your mentor?" Jeremiah had always said he didn't care about my submission but now there was a fork in the road.

By now, Jeremiah aroused my suspicion. After almost two decades of friendship, mentorship and business partnership, I no longer felt he understood me or considered my best interests. When our family of seven moved across the country for his business, living out of suitcases in a one-bedroom apartment, he didn't even invite us over for dinner. "I don't think we're a good fit." "My wife has an issue with…" "I think our ministries should be separated…". At first I believed his excuses. I think partly because he believed them and partly because I believed I was the problem. But what made his mixed motives the most obvious were our business dealings.

Jeremiah said he didn't care about money, but all of our business meetings seemed to go his way. I constantly heard about meetings he had with others behind my back that didn't seem to line up with what I heard when we talked face to face. Regardless of my suspicions, I knew I still needed to submit, especially for an accusation of this magnitude. I told him I would discuss my pride with him but only if my five closest friends and church leaders were present.

One week later we met. It was four days before Christmas in 2015. Kami was eight months pregnant with our 6th child. Jeremiah presented a five page document that detailed his concerns with my pride and how it was destructive to me and the community. It said:

Ben has a pattern of domineering and unsubmissive pride. He gravitates toward projects that place himself at the center and result in him getting the glory, not God.

The nature of our community was that our friends were also our business partners, neighbors, and spiritual leaders. Our brand of fundamentalism was a 24/7 lifestyle and we only trusted people to do business with that had similar ideas as us. My best friend, who I had gone on to start the blackjack website with, had been our neighbor and business partner. The co-owners and other board members of the storytelling advertising business included Jeremiah and other religious leaders. This meant that these accusations were not just something I could walk away from.

Sitting around the table, Jeremiah and the other leaders all agreed: this was a serious matter; one that had serious consequences and one I needed to seek God's will on. They all agreed that I would not be able to seek God's will about pride while drawing attention to myself on vlog episodes so I would need to take a week off.

I had stuck with my schedule, publishing 56 vlog episodes on time, and knew I shouldn't quit. But I also knew that Christians need to submit to authority and these were my friends that had my best interest in mind. I wanted to prove that I still cared about God and was committed. Plus, if I didn't listen, I would be guilty of rebellion and pride, proving my accusers right. Knowing that the salvation of my soul was more important than my self expression, I decided to submit to my spiritual leaders and friends instead of the schedule I had created for myself.

I went home. It was difficult to talk about it with Kami. Jeremiah was her older brother and she had always looked up to him. Kami had never really felt comfortable with the vlog and had only really supported it because I was so adamant about needing to do it. Now questions came up in her mind. Her family had accused her of being brainwashed and too close to me and the situation to be objective. This pride, or narcissism, or whatever it was, if left unchecked, would not just hurt me, the community, and her, but she was pregnant with our 6th child and extra vulnerable. While Jeremiah and the other community members were not able to recommend a divorce, they were warning her in every way they could. Kami didn't have the confidence to stand up when everyone we knew was saying the same thing. She started to question if maybe she had enabled me too much and if going along with my ideas was getting us all in trouble. After the meeting, she cried all night.

That night Jeremiah sent me a text, "I know that was hard but I'm proud of you. You did the right thing."

Then, I took a week off.

Another Week

After taking a week off, I checked in with Jeremiah and the other leaders with a list of my conclusions. I did find pride and admitted to them a list of my findings along with what I proposed to change. They looked at my list skeptically but had a more pressing issue. Even though I hadn't filmed, edited or published any videos like they had asked and had spent six hours a day in prayer, reading the Bible, and meditating, they saw that I had made a post on Instagram during that week. They agreed that this was prideful and a sign that I should take another week off. I agreed because I thought if I jumped through one more hoop I would make them happy and prove my commitment. I didn't realize there would be no end to the hoops. Deep down I wondered if the vlog would ever continue or whether I would go back to being depressed and crazy.

More Sin

After that week passed, the leaders begrudgingly let me return to vlogging. But they said that my pride still needed to be dealt with. Every week I returned for another assignment. I met with Jeremiah and the other leaders. My best friend, who started the blackjack team and website, wouldn't talk to me directly anymore. He said all communication needed to go through the church leaders. I felt like a registered sex offender living across the street from a daycare. I felt like cancer.

Eventually, I sold my blackjack training website to my best friend because the leaders demanded it and I thought it would make things better. I didn't want to sell it but the spiritual leaders said I must stop being prideful and let them broker the deal. I had stopped sleeping at night and was so worn out that I sold my 50% of the business and let my old partner choose the price. I think I lost six figures on the deal but I just wanted to be done and prove I could submit. At least I had my main source of income, the advertising business, left.

Our YouTube channel had stalled out at 82 subscribers. Each video still took eight hours to publish, was only getting around 30 views, wasn't making any money and wasn't changing anyone's life. I wondered if it was all worth it. I was locked into an unending spiritual discipline process as a consequence of creating a vlog that didn't benefit my life or anyone else's.

My Last Friend

I walked two doors down to my close friend and asked his advice. I wanted to know if he thought I should try and recover the business relationships with my church friends (that had made me millions) by quitting the vlog and apologizing. Or, pour my life into a YouTube channel that had 82 subscribers and hadn't made any money, and pursue my dream of writing a book without an agent or publisher. I had met with this friend at 6 a.m. for years and trusted his opinion. The decision felt like life or death. My friend asked, "Do you really want to know what I think?"

"Of course," I said. And I really did.

They say to flip a coin with important decisions because when the coin is in the air you know how you want it to land. When the coin is in the air, you get clarity in what it is you really want.

While I sat there waiting for my friend's answer, for the first time I knew what I wanted him to say. But he came back with the opposite.

"You're not a writer. The business that you have with Jeremiah is the best thing you have going for you. You've made a ton of money and these guys really care for you. Over the last ten years you guys have built something most people only dream about. It would be foolish to walk away."

I told my friend thank you for his advice, that it was really valuable.

Then I walked home.

I never talked to him again.

<u>My 85th Video</u>

It had been 15 years since we had our first child, Dove — the birth we had invited eight people to. At that time, Jeremiah had warned me about how dangerous it was to expose others to the graphic nature of birth. This warning had changed my life as I became afraid to share parts of our sexuality, excitement, shadow self or anything else that wasn't commonly public. At that time, I had lost all confidence in myself or my ability to help others. But now, things were different. I had been in SA for six years, shared my darkest moments with hundreds and gotten feedback that my story had helped people. And so now, with the birth of our sixth child coming up, and our comfort of sharing our lives on video increasing, the birth felt like something I had to film.

Kami gave birth in our attic and there were tears, nudity, and insane animal grunting sounds. Reviewing the video footage, I saw my wife screaming, the kids crying, and a group of people huddled around an inflatable tub as a bloody baby came out. It was a boy and we named him Rainier after our favorite mountain in Washington.

While the church leadership had technically reinstated permission to vlog, I was very much in a probationary period. I thought about Jeremiah's criticism and how our first birth had made family members uncomfortable. I thought about how I had been accused of compromising my wife's dignity and how I had sacrificed our ability to work at Bible camp by publishing one small confession of being a sexaholic. I thought about the friends, leaders, and family that had accused me of being reckless, dangerous and prideful. I thought about Jeremiah's recent accusation from two months earlier:

"He gravitates toward projects that place himself at the center and result in him getting the glory, not God." I knew, to these people, publishing Rainier's birth on YouTube would be just another way to get attention. Another reckless move not only endangering Kami but my own salvation. But if I wasn't willing to publish the material that moved me the most, what was the point? I had to choose.

Rainier's birth video would be impossible to ignore. Publishing it would have ramifications. There was no way around this and once published, there was no going back. This could mean losing the friendships and family I had spent the last 35 years investing in.

But, as I spent two full days editing the video (with a newborn), I saw magic. I saw the miracle of birth, I saw the strength of Kami, I saw the reactions of our children when they welcomed their new brother and I saw a piece of art that could change people's perspectives on family, medicine, and humanity. It was true, it was immodest, but it was honest, and it was the piece of work I was the most proud of. Just like what I discovered in the basement of SA, I simply could not keep it to myself. I watched it over and over and wanted my friends to see it. A birth like Rainier's was something I had never seen online. It felt selfish to hoard it.

I looked over at Kami who was holding Rainier, just two days old. She had been through cycles, wondering if maybe the leaders and her family were right. Maybe I had pride. Maybe she was brainwashed. She may have been enabling me. She wasn't sure about a lot of these things. What she was sure about was that she trusted me and she, too, believed Rainier's birth was amazing and worth sharing. She had gone to her own 12-step groups and worked through hangups about nudity and modesty that required self-censorship. We looked at each other.

I waited.

She smiled and nodded.

This was our moment.

I clicked publish.

I had just violated the most important unwritten rule of our community in the boldest way. We had just shared our most raw and intimate moment on the largest platform on the planet.

I'm Not A Monster

Because of our continuation of the vlog, the publication of Rainier's birth video, and the apparent lack of progress, the church leaders were pissed. While I was following their directions, they could see I wasn't giving them the fear and respect they wanted. Soon they came back with another list of sins. This one was bigger than the last one. They said I needed to find a therapist who would help with my pride because my problems were too big for them.

This was a kick in the gut. I had to go through the phonebook, find someone who was supposed to fix me and pay for it out-of-pocket. I didn't think it would be helpful but after investing two years and losing hundreds of thousands of dollars, I made the mistake of hoping that one more step of obedience would win the leaders over. Plus, I was out of options and thought maybe I could learn something new.

The website said Johnson and Associates. At the top of the list was Tom Johnson -- the most expensive. $170 for 50 minutes. I chose him, thinking I might as well speed up the process with the most qualified guy. I called him Boss Tom.

Boss Tom had short-styled gray hair, a hoop earring and wore really smart and sophisticated looking glasses. He was intelligent, open-minded and, just like in SA meetings, I felt like nothing I could say would scare or surprise him. Boss Tom specialized in church trauma — something I didn't even know existed. And what I learned from him was inspiring but disruptive. At first, I wanted to believe the accusations about my pride because it was the easiest way to be restored to the community. I would just find out where I had made mistakes, apologize, fix my shit, and move the fuck on. But Boss Tom had other ideas.

My time in therapy started to replace my SA meetings. Originally, I attended SA because I thought I needed healing from an addiction. Over eight years, I started new meetings, hosted meetings in my house, went to conferences and eventually sponsored people myself. But now I could see that what I really valued from SA was a safe place for connection which I was now finding by meeting with a therapist.

When I contacted my sponsor, William, to get his take on transitioning out of SA, I was worried. William was a lifer and the literature was clear: one does not get cured of sexaholism. The only solution is to commit to the program for life. His response startled me, "I never thought you were a real sexaholic anyway."

Talking to Boss Tom was the only time of the week I felt normal. So I doubled down on meetings and started booking two sessions back to back. In one of our first meetings, Boss Tom said he didn't observe any narcissism or pride in me but just an "exaggerated need for intimacy and expression." I called Kami on the drive home from that appointment and said, "I don't think I'm a monster." Both of us were crying.

·

The Last Straw

I was mandated to go to therapy to become more compliant. The plan backfired. Instead, I started finding confidence and learning to stand up for myself for the first time in my life. I originally saw therapy as punishment but now Kami started coming with me to all of the therapy sessions and we treated it like a date. We would go sit with Boss Tom for two hours, asking questions, tearing down our convictions on religion and our relationship and then we would go and eat cupcakes, just staring at each other wondering how we were to go back to the kids and parent like functioning adults.

Boss Tom helped us unravel what had happened to us. We were confused because we trusted the leaders and the words they said, but Boss Tom taught us how to look at people's actions. While the leaders said everything they did was because they loved us, we felt accused, abandoned, and devastated by how we were treated.

I had always blamed myself for the discrepancy between how I felt and what those in spiritual authority said, but he said the discipline process I was going through sounded like spiritual abuse. He said the people who seemed so confident in accusing me were the ones with pride, not me who was open to change. He said that hierarchies of power that control people always cause hurt and result in a stream of destruction. In fact, he said that many of the clients he had were a result of the same church leaders who had hurt us.

Now I started to look at the leadership differently. I had always trusted them, but now I could see a wake of carnage and broken relationships in their past. I even started to meet with people who had just disappeared from the community and I heard stories that validated what Boss Tom was saying.

I could see there was another side of the coin in what I was now starting to see as a fundamentalist cult. We were more concerned with control than love and our standards of purity and holy living were more about our own comfort than they were about helping others or making God happy.
I was ready to repent, but not of pride. I was ready to repent for prioritizing my own certainty and stubbornness over having an open mind, for labeling and excluding people for my own comfort, and for promoting hierarchical structures that hurt people.

I wanted the church leaders to hear Boss Tom's perspective so we could all learn together. This information could help us love God and each other better. I proposed that the church leaders meet with Boss Tom and I offered to pay for it. He met with both leaders.

"How'd it go," I eagerly asked.

"About how I expected it to go. They're not interested in my opinion and don't want to meet again."

The leaders were more interested in control and the well-being of the system they had created than love, connection, or even obedience to God.

But Kami and I continued to put the work in, studying cults, systems of oppression and coercion and eventually writing an apology letter to 18 different families we had interacted with over the years. We viewed this as progress and a sign that we were healing and growing. The church leaders saw it as rebellion. They asked for a copy of the letter and when they found out I was apologizing for the ways we had abused hierarchy but not for pride, it was the last straw. They had lost control of me.

I could see that no amount of time or obedience would make these leaders happy. They wanted something I couldn't give them. They wanted me to be quiet. They wanted me to agree. They wanted me to respect a system of silence and compliance that had almost destroyed me and my family.

I had spent 30 years in the church trying to convince people and two years in a spiritual discipline process that had drained our family and finances all to prove how committed I was to the group that I cared about more than anything else on the planet. And after all that, I was going to lose it all.

Excommunication

I wish I could tell you that I was brave and walked away from the leadership that was destroying my life, that I concluded I didn't need the people I had surrounded myself with — who my therapist called "damaged." But, I still needed these people. It was too painful to let go. Instead of bravely walking away, I would go through a much longer and painful process of getting dumped and then having the equivalent of restraining orders filed on my ass as I begged to be let back into the relationship.

I found out I had been excommunicated at a coffee shop. I bumped into my friend Mark and said "hi." Mark was 6 foot 4 inches, always wore shorts, a Patagonia hat and Chaco sandals regardless if it was summer or if there was snow on the ground. He said, "I'll make this quick. I met with the leaders. I'm not going to be talking to you anymore. And I'm going to tell everyone I know not to talk to you either." He stated it very matter-of-factly.

I was stunned. I had hired Mark as my blackjack team manager. We had climbed mountains and road-tripped across the country. I had trusted him with hundreds of thousands of dollars and he had lived in my home with my children. Now, it was over.

At first, I was confused. I had taken the ordered week off, and then another, and had jumped through every hoop I knew to jump through. I had followed every written rule they had communicated. It would be years before I would get clear communication about the crime I committed. It would come from Jeremiah in the form of a letter addressed to Kami that simply said the Bible verses in 2 Timothy 3: 1-9 described who I was. We looked them up:

> *…There will be terrible times in the last days. People will be lovers of themselves, lovers of money, boastful, proud, abusive, disobedient to their parents, ungrateful, unholy, without love, unforgiving, slanderous, without self-control, brutal, not lovers of the good, treacherous, rash, conceited, lovers of pleasure rather than lovers of God… Have nothing to do with such people. They are the kind who worm their way into homes and gain control over gullible women, who are loaded down with sins and are swayed by all kinds of evil desires, always learning but never able to come to a knowledge of the truth.…these teachers oppose the truth. They are men of depraved minds…*

We were confused. By now I had run the gamut of trying to make sense of my unusual behaviors and had dabbled with explanations that included narcissism, autism, neurodivergence, and having an Asian mom. Gaining control of gullible women didn't make any sense to either of us. But there was no conversation, court hearing, or evidence, and it didn't matter. The sentence was being carried out.

We stopped getting invited to family functions. Soon after, I got a message from a newly hired board member saying I had one week to sell the shares of my advertising business, my primary source of income. If I didn't sell my shares, they would be re-evaluated at the discretion of my "friends."

Replaceable (A New Perspective)

During my years in church, I had seen many people disappear. When I was on the inside, I told myself that it was the fault of those who disappeared. *They* made bad choices, *they* were rebellious, or *they* walked away. Now I was the one being replaced.

Wanting to believe that the friendships I had fostered for decades were real, I kept on thinking that one of my old friends that had always applauded me for my intelligence and courage would come to me and ask me what we were learning or what new information had changed our beliefs — that they would want to hear my side of the story. It never happened. The second we stopped playing a role that propped up their belief system, they started looking for someone else and others stepped in overnight. Friends that I had known for decades and lived on my block and had even been present at Rainier's birth, quietly moved away without even saying goodbye and even started to go to Bible studies at Jeremiah's house. As far as Jeremiah, my brother-in-law, business partner and mentor of 20 years was concerned, he said he needed a year off from any communication with me and Kami — his sister.

Shunned

A close friend told us she had received a letter warning about us, saying that we were shunned but to keep it a secret from us. Another friend, who had helped us start our YouTube channel and was planning on starting a podcast with us, said Jeremiah had reached out and warned him. Now he didn't want to move forward with the podcast. We had lost our way of making money and now Jeremiah was going to others, warning them not to do business with me. Our savings would only last so long. I started to get paranoid.

In our old church system, we were not just neutral outsiders that had lost our membership, we were seen as dangerous. Now that I could no longer offer peace of mind to my friends, my existence threatened their security. I was seen as an enemy like someone who had switched teams.

After more than two years of sacrificing our money and time, and trying to do everything that was asked of us so that we could be accepted and fit in, I was called rebellious, unsubmissive, and told that I didn't even try. I could see that being on the other team meant the facts didn't matter. After three decades of arranging my entire life around building and protecting my reputation, it was gone and I had nothing to show for it.

The pain and confusion of losing all of my friends caused me to live in constant guilt and regret. I was waking up in the middle of the night, gaining weight, and afraid to leave my house. I had no vision for a way forward and no alternate belief system to turn to. Our only friend was Boss Tom who charged us $170 a session and said if he saw us at a party, he wouldn't acknowledge us for confidentiality reasons.

I believed that the church leaders had made a mistake. Someday my oppressors would apologize when they understood all the facts. It was my job to be patient and faithful until that day. I had simply invested too much to believe my reputation, trust, and community could all just vanish. Waiting on the doorstep like a lonely and eager puppy wanting to be let in and wanting to help the truth get out faster, I would become more extreme and fundamentalist — the strategy that had always worked in the past. Our family started taking Hebrew lessons five days a week and made plans to move to the Holy Land, the epicenter of holiness. Following God became more important than ever.

5: The Benefit
Sharing's Reward

Walking It Off On The A.T.

Even though I wanted to wait indefinitely, things were working inside of me that made this impossible. I couldn't unsee what I had seen. I didn't want to evolve but seeing a new part of the church was making me change in ways I had never imagined. A baby can't re-enter the womb and a caterpillar can't crawl back into the cocoon.

I had always considered myself a free-thinker but with all of my friends gone, I could see I had underestimated the role that they played and the security they provided. In our Christian community, some of Boss Tom's advice would have been questionable, but now he was our only friend and he was giving us permission to explore new thoughts and ideas. Views we used to consider heretical or dangerous, now, all of a sudden, started to make sense. We could hear things for the first time.

With my body still covered in Christian tattoos, I started to re-examine beliefs that I had held my entire life. I had developed layers onto my belief system but the basis of it had been established almost four decades earlier at the age of four (based on a fear of hell). These beliefs had been set in cement, without re-examination since.

Boss Tom asked a lot of questions. He challenged my view of masturbation being a sin and always harmful. He told us stories and made us re-think our disgust of divorce. I learned that the very same Bible passages that had helped me were also used to hurt people. I could also see that I had been very selective about which Bible verses I memorized and had only focused on the passages that helped me, that brought me certainty, and made me feel superior.

Now that I no longer felt the drive for certainty or superiority, the Bible was less helpful for daily guidance. Black and white prohibitions, like avoiding sex before marriage and not swearing, partying, or doing drugs, all felt a little ridiculous. The guidelines I had based my entire life on felt shallow and haphazard.

These changes felt foreign and very difficult to integrate. We had spent our entire lives oriented around people; how to save them, how to lead them, and how to serve them, and now they were all gone. This space created pain but also opportunity. We found ourselves with open schedules for the first time in our adult lives. Wanting to fulfill a lifelong dream and now needing to get away, our family decided to spend five months walking through the woods on the Appalachian Trail. On the trail, we befriended hundreds of other hikers and people who offered us meals, laundry, and lodging. For the first time in my life, I didn't care what anyone believed. I wasn't trying to save anyone. If you were walking the same path, willing to talk to my kids, offered us potato chips or a shower, you were an equal. You were a friend.

The kids found most of the trail difficult and the friendships we created made it bearable. But our main motivation for finishing the trail faster than was thought possible was to make it to our old Bible camp to cook. The leadership had changed and it seemed like everyone had moved on from the fear of me being a sex addict. This made Bible camp one of the few places from our previous life we were still welcome. Originally we thought we would not be able to make it to camp and hike the trail in the same summer, but on day four, huddled in a cabin under frozen rain, our kids barfing and everyone wanting to quit, we hatched an impossible plan with the prize: a week at Bible camp. The goal motivated our family to average 13.5 miles every day (more than a half marathon) for five months straight, including a 53 day stretch with no days off. It was all worth it when we arrived at Bible camp heroes, able to rest, reunited with friends and family, making my famous Liege-style waffles in the kitchen for 200 people. I even gave a slideshow in the chapel of our adventure and what we learned about family and parenting. It was good to be home. The feeling wouldn't last.

No Rules

Returning home after hiking for five months was a difficult transition. On the trail we were distracted from the fact that we had lost all of our community. When we got back home, the reminder that we were alone hit us in the face. After six months away, our way of relating together as a family had changed. After our time partnering with our kids to accomplish a 2,000 mile goal most said was impossible, it felt weird going back to our military, top-down, parenting style. We decided to change things up.

Kami and I wanted to learn to listen to our kids but we were not able to act like cops and listen to them at the same time. We needed a detox from the controlling authoritarianism that defined our parenting. On January 1, 2019, we announced to our kids that we were going to do a year without rules. Some of our kids were excited and others were nervous. Rules were the way we operated and overnight we were tossing them all out. No one knew what was going to happen.

Immediately chaos ensued. Dishes piled up and our oldest boy stayed up till 4 a.m. playing video games. At first, we were overwhelmed by the loss of normalcy, but something much deeper was happening. As our kids stopped doing the things that rules mandated, we started to see that our kids' obedience was motivated by fear, not agreement. They would do what we wanted and listen to our advice because they had to. Our relationship was based upon an authority role. We learned from our church friends that these roles are very fragile and once either of us stopped playing the role, if the relationship was based upon submission, it would be over. We wanted to figure out another way to connect to our kids — a way that would last.

Creating A Safe Space

Disagreement was something we had never seen in our home. It was never allowed. Our kids always agreed, or at least acted like it. Any disagreements were hidden. For my kids to feel safe, they needed a dad who listened. A dad who heard them and accepted them for who they are. A dad who focused on them, not the rules I thought were important.

I had learned that the more a place calls itself "safe," the more dangerous it is. In church and home, dissension was viewed as a failure, with threats ranging from "burning in hell" and "learning the hard way" to actual consequences like being shunned. This meant that home and church were only safe as long as you agreed. There was one place I had felt safe in my life to share anything — SA. SA was a place I felt accepted and known, where rules and disagreement didn't matter.

I proposed a weekly 12-step meeting where family members could share their struggles and failures just like I had done. The kids looked at me skeptically. They had never been to an SA meeting and were used to being judged for their mistakes.

The first meeting was rough. Listening without judgment was a new thing for us parents and it didn't seem natural to share as equals. I had worn the cop hat for so long in the relationship, it was all I knew. Our first meeting was awkwardly silent. We opened the time for sharing and no one said anything. The kids were scared to speak, worried they would be punished or shamed if they said anything real. They had only seen the consequences of vulnerability in our home and none of the benefits. The kids intuitively knew our home wasn't safe.

I wanted to change this. In order to do that I would have to lead. But not by ordering that they share. I would lead by example. I would lead with weakness.

Contagious

"Instead of writing my book, I wasted time on internet sites for two hours and then felt like shit afterward." I didn't give the kids a moral of the story, I didn't tie anything up with a bow or Bible verse, and I didn't act like the strong parent or role model. I just shared honestly.

The kids squirmed uncomfortably. Some of them started to giggle and they looked at each other but then tried to avoid eye contact, knowing they might burst into laughter. No one responded.

When I first started sharing authentically, I was concerned about the negative impact it would have on my kids. I thought they would lose respect for me or copy my failures, no longer having a good example. The first few meetings it was just Kami and me sharing. The kids stayed silent except for the giggling and scripted reading. But sharing about my failures wasn't causing our kids to fail more, it was helping them feel less alone in the failure they were already experiencing. Instead of losing respect, the opposite happened. After two awkwardly short meetings, a breakthrough happened in our third meeting as a kid spoke up and shared.

"I slept in this week."

And then another one spoke up:

"I ate so much candy I got a stomach ache."

As a parent, remaining silent was a lot easier to do with strangers who I didn't feel responsibility toward but just like SA, we all agreed to "no cross talk." So I just sat back and listened. With no advice, no critique, just a "thank you for sharing," the amount of sharing and vulnerability started to increase.

"I played video games and watched YouTube for four hours and didn't finish my projects."

"Thank you for sharing."

"I miss our cousins. It's not fair we're not invited to family parties."

"Thank you for sharing."

In our living room at our weekly 12 step meeting, I was hearing things I had never heard before. I always wanted my kids to be vulnerable with me but was never able to achieve that by demanding it. Now that we were modeling it, the kids saw it and wanted it themselves. They now openly discussed their love lives, something they had never done when we were constantly judging and offering advice. We just listened and said "thanks for sharing."

Eventually their boldness started to spill over to other platforms. The kids started to become more expressive on their social media and in the way they dressed. When our family entered the limelight for various controversies, it was my two teenage daughters that asked to record vlogs speaking up against ignorant haters and writing public letters to Olympic athletes and celebrities. My kids who were once fearful, quiet and subdued were now becoming my partners in crime, inspiring me with their honesty, boldness, and unique angles. Kami was changing, too. She started taking music lessons, singing in front of others and even writing songs as a way to process her feelings of pain.

The increased vulnerability was not always easy. Some of the kids' pain was from our strict parenting and choices. And Kami felt safe to open up about ways she had felt threatened and oppressed in the first decade of our sexual relationship.

Instead of silencing the kids and Kami, or judging them, I just listened and tried to understand. While sometimes the truth stung, the benefits of being open to it were worth it. Instead of focusing on all of the ways we were different as parents, I was able to see the ways we were the same. It started to feel less lonely for me *and* for them. I started to relate to them and through my sharing, they were able to relate to me. New connections started happening in our family that we had never seen before. But now, we started to see bigger obstacles that were making connection impossible.

Judgment Kills Connection

Learning a new way to relate made me realize that 90% of my thoughts and writings were judgmental statements:

> Kids *should* do the dishes instead of leaving a mess on the counter.
>
> Kids *shouldn't* stay up till 4 a.m. playing video games.
>
> People *shouldn't* do drugs or have sex before marriage.
>
> People *should* take off their shoes in my house.

"Should" or statements like "this way of life is better than that way of life" are statements of judgment. There are thousands of variations of these judgmental thoughts.

What judgmental thoughts and statements have in common:

1. They put me on a pedestal as if I know more or follow the code better than others.

2. They are condescending.

3. They create classes and separation in society based upon our ability to measure up to the code.

4. The codes I subscribed to had always been uninteresting to others! This is why Republicans don't care what Democrats think and Christians are not curious what Hindus think and, of course, why kids don't give a shit about what adults think.

> 5. The main way judgments are implemented is by force, hierarchy, and control.

The judgments I made toward my children provided the basis for the preaching/teaching/advice I gave them. I wasn't doing this because it was effective, I was preaching because it was the only way I knew to relate to children. And now that these methods were disappearing, we needed another way to connect with our children, outside of our weekly meetings. Our house was still more chaotic than ever, living with no rules, and we needed a new way to parent.

The Power To Connect

According to Marshall Rosenberg, author of *Nonviolent Communication*, every judgment comes out of an unmet need. At first, this sounded like a load of pop psych victimized bullshit. But I had been hurt by enough judgments that I was curious to understand.

Sharing about personal needs and desires was scary for me. I had never done it and thought it was prideful and sinful. All we talked about was what God wanted. Owning desires was vulnerable and left me open to rejection. This is why it had always been easier to create rules in our house and act as if they were universal or "common sense."

We had used our authority to hide behind these rules, but with no rules in 2019, I couldn't hide anymore. I was getting more and more pissed about the dishes piling up around the sink and my oldest boy playing video games till 4 a.m. and I didn't know how to deal with it.

It took all of the tools I had gotten in SA and therapy to figure out how me being pissed about dishes and all-night video games translated to unmet needs. At first, it felt like a stretch. But eventually, I could see I was using rules and asking the kids to change their behavior because I wasn't willing to face parts of myself.

When I finally sat down to share, my palms were sweaty. The kids' small size didn't make opening up less scary. I told the kids that having dishes stacked high felt chaotic, which made me feel unsafe and insecure. They shared that they felt the same way. Turns out, they wanted the dishes done as much as I did. So, we came up with a schedule that we all agreed upon. The results were very different from demanding the kids do the dishes because it was "their job." Now, it felt like we all wanted the same goal — like we were all in this together. My vulnerability had paved the way for a mutual struggle having a joint solution.

Next up was my son's late night video game habit. The tricky part would be sharing honestly and vulnerably, without manipulation. I would need to let the results go and accept him either way. I shared that watching him stay up late made me feel like a bad parent. I believed bed times were important and video games were a waste of time. I wanted him to be making money or reading books or writing letters or something else more prestigious than killing fake aliens. His response surprised me. Instead of getting defensive, he shared that he had been struggling with the same thing. He wanted to go to bed early and didn't know how. He struggled with productivity and feeling overwhelmed with making money.

Instead of being condescending from a pedestal, I shared how I felt the same way and felt like a failure for not being a published author by the age of 40. Now, instead of feeling like a cop, I felt like an ally. I didn't have to act like I was on a pedestal and he didn't have to defend his actions from an inferior position. My sharing had created a bond that made each of us feel less lonely.

Not long after this conversation, I noticed the video games ending earlier and earlier. Choosing access to my son and earning his trust was better than enforcing my arbitrary goals, and the irony was that it helped with my goals, as well. I thought about the reading I had heard every week in SA:

> *"Many of us felt inadequate, unworthy, alone, and afraid. Our insides never matched what we saw on the outsides of others. Early on, we came to feel disconnected--from parents, from peers, from ourselves."*

By sharing, I had made my son feel less alone. Both of our needs were getting met. I was breaking a cycle. Maybe real power wasn't being the one who created and enforced the rules but being the one who could let the rules go to connect with those I loved.

__Exvangelical__

The year after we hiked the Appalachian Trail, I spent most of my time writing a book about our experience called *2000 Miles Together*. I also started to discover podcasts and books in a new category called "exvangelical" where I heard many stories just like mine. The exact situations were different but the main themes were always the same: control, exclusion, coercion. Often the people who were the most devoted were the ones who found themselves on the outside the quickest. There were many examples of how devotion, honesty, and passion had been turned around on someone and used as a weapon to hurt them when they stopped complying. I started researching cults, high-control groups, and brainwashing. Our communities were free of membership, kool-aid and formal agreements, so I thought we were exempt. In a podcast about cults, I heard a list of eight prevalent indicators of brainwashing. Our group contained seven them.

I had always thought of cults as these weird obvious groups somewhere out there. Now I started to see cults as a spectrum, a range of practices that used control and coercion to create a false sense of unity. A group that leveraged inclusion to get people to conform. When I started to recognize these indicators, I started to see them everywhere. I had used these techniques to parent my children and to exclude those who weren't convenient for me. And now that we no longer fit into our spiritual "family" these same techniques were being used against us.

These techniques were great at creating a false sense of unity for the short term. But they always came at the price of the individual's health and therefore always fell apart in the long term. Now I could see that I didn't choose my beliefs of my own free will. I had hung on to them for survival. You don't get to choose what you believe when the beliefs are dependent upon you being cared for. But now, for the first time in my life, I let go and felt that I would survive.

For the first time in my life I started to question the core beliefs that had motivated me since I was four. Instead of certainty — the thing that had motivated me to wear Christian t-shirts every day, want to be a missionary, and alienate all of my relationships through preaching, I started to say that maybe I didn't know the answer. Maybe I didn't need to. I started to embrace curiosity. These changes showed on the outside. I started to grow my hair out, something I had always wanted to do but felt guilty for. I got my hands tattooed - another dream but something I felt would draw too much attention and distract from God's message. And I started experimenting with psychedelics, something I had deemed only for selfish partiers and people who didn't take life seriously.

Our old communities would have seen these activities as just trying to get attention. The irony for me was that the opposite was true. The community was where I sought attention and for the first time in my life, I was just trying to be me. These changes felt like an honest reflection of what was going on inside of me. Instead of fabricating for others, I started to write about things I felt — the things that made me angry and kept me up at night. I didn't know how others would receive them but I didn't care. I was putting my oxygen mask on first.

Stockholm Syndrome

Even though I had shared my parenting failures and entire sexual inventory with the world, there was one glaring topic I was silent on: my excommunication and the way my Christian friends had treated us.

I cared more about protecting the reputation of my abusers than I did my own reputation. Stockholm syndrome is real. I had protected the system for so long that it was still easier to blame myself for my excommunication. Even though I had been ambushed, slandered, shunned, and excommunicated, I felt guilty about what had happened to me. I felt like I deserved it and that it was my job to quietly disappear.

I was meticulous about who I talked to, making sure not to gossip, and was super careful about what I said, only sharing facts and painting the leadership in the best possible light. I kept names and details silent, insisting that the motives of my abusers and those who had excommunicated us were good.

But at night I laid awake, staring at the ceiling, running the facts around in my head again and again. It simply didn't make sense. If I was this bad and dangerous, why was I such a respected leader for decades? Had I changed overnight or was the organization I had pledged my life to not what I thought? What did it even matter if none of the people I wanted to convince would listen?

You Own Your Story

I was on my way to having PTSD. I've talked to many people who are surprised that I'm still able to talk and function after what we've been through. I have two explanations for this speedy recovery. One was the heavy use of therapeutic psychedelics. The second was my commitment to publicly share every detail about what happened.

The vague nature of my abuse made it especially difficult to recover from. Vagueness favors those with power. My shunning lacked honest or specific communication. I was not told what I did, who I was shunned from, who would know about it, how long it would last, or when it would end. I experienced anxiety any time I went outside, afraid of bumping into someone at the grocery store. I was nervous about being honest on social media now, not knowing what they were thinking or how I would be treated. Not having an official accusation or penalty meant that my mind was always running, trying to fill in the gaps of what had happened and how I should navigate the world. This took an incredible amount of energy and time, and created more pain as I relived the most painful experiences again and again trying to make sense of my life and what had happened. The excommunication was painful but the stories I was creating in my mind, in the absence of honest communication, were even more painful.

I spent hours sifting through what was said and done. I would play the scenes over and over like a tape recorder but with no change. Kami and I would repeat the same stories again and again. We had shared our facts with Boss Tom but having one outside witness only went so far. If I was going to re-engage in society, be able to sleep at night, or ever be an author, I needed healing. I needed to process my trauma. I needed to know what I was guilty of and how to change or I needed to know that the system was rigged and I had been fucked.

My abusers had silenced me by slamming my reputation. They said that any sharing I did of my excommunication was "wallowing," "belaboring the point," or "spiteful revenge." They said I needed to forgive and move on but now I could see that my silence was only protecting them, not me or the truth.
I learned in SA that I don't need a reputation to share. I just need my story and the courage to share it. Even though the facts were on my side I had always been afraid to open up. I had been meticulous about saving timelines, emails, and even recordings of all the meetings (including our therapy sessions).

But talking about how I had been hurt still felt like playing the victim. It still felt wrong to be talking shit about people who we thought meant well. And then I came across a writing by Anne Lamott that said, "You own everything that happened to you…if people wanted you to write warmly about them, they should've behaved better." I decided I needed to prioritize my own health and that I wasn't willing to take responsibility for other parties not doing the work. I needed to discuss the facts around my pain because I wanted trauma to be minimized in my life and the lives of my children.

I wasn't going to get any validation from my community, but I could validate myself. Publishing an honest story says "this happened," "this opinion is real," and "this opinion is just as valid as the group's." The people who were wanting me to move on weren't really wanting me to move on, they were just wanting me to be silent, something I was no longer willing to do. I learned in SA that when it comes to shame, it's only when you can fully embrace every detail of your history that it really can be history. To move on, I needed to hear the truth and if no one else was going to say it out loud, I would have to say it myself.

I was finally ready to tell my story. All of it.

<u>My Share</u>

The first podcast episode I recorded about how I had been excommunicated, I was shaking. I had gone over my notes, timelines, emails, and audio recordings. It was all of my evidence for the court case I wanted with my friends. I felt misrepresented and misunderstood. I had waited years for them to come and ask me my side of the story or see my evidence, but the phone calls never came. Their courtroom was rigged and my story would never be heard there. But I didn't need it anymore. By sharing my story I was creating my own.

Every detail I shared on my podcast released me from resentment, bondage, and the guilt that I had held. It made me less crazy. These details may not have been interesting to my audience or essential for the story but they were essential to me. I was un-gaslighting myself. Every secret I kept was an endorsement of a system that had almost killed me. Keeping other people's secrets stunted my growth and progress more than I knew. Every secret I held made me question my sanity and validity as a human. The way we made sense of outsiders' stories when I was in the church was by telling ourselves they were selfish or they were less intelligent. Each of our judgments and beliefs was a bar of a cage that we built to contain them. Now I was an outsider trapped in the very cage I helped build. Each detail I shared felt like a bar being removed. It started in my therapist's office. Just saying the words out loud by yourself for another human is sometimes enough. But for some of us, it takes more. I wanted to be an author. I had to share my story publicly. As publicly as I had shared my faith.

Over ten podcast episodes, I shared every detail that I had meticulously documented. Kami sat by my side for every episode, too. Many of the things that had happened to us had been too painful to discuss with each other but now we were facing the facts of what had happened together. With the motivation of the podcast, we had ten uninterrupted hours of just processing and listening to each other. We weren't trying to hurt anyone, but we were done protecting them, too. We didn't know how the world was going to respond and for the first time we didn't care.

Burning Down The House

As soon as the podcast was released, people I hadn't heard from in years reached out to me, telling me they were concerned about the accuracy of my story and wanting to help me by offering a few corrections. All of a sudden, people "cared." As predicted, their advice was that I should stop dwelling and "move on."

Where were all of these motherfuckers the last two years while I was almost dead? I learned a lot from the timing of when people responded. As long as I was quiet, I didn't hear from anyone. But the second we spoke up, people had to reckon with our existence and why we didn't fit in their tribe anymore. They weren't concerned with the details or facts. They were trying to keep their own beliefs intact and couldn't justify the incongruency of what had happened to us.

Certain friends took it upon themselves to correct my heretical opinions by posing challenging or insightful questions, always playing devil's advocate. They claimed to be "protecting" me from "danger." They said I had run into a few bad apples and I should give God and church another chance. At first, I politely engaged, but soon enough I could see that no matter how polite I was, there was no real conversation. Even though they typed question marks, they were not actually curious.

John, the friend and old business partner who was making Bible videos and had offered to coach me on YouTube, left a two star review on the podcast titled: "Burning Down the House." I was thankful for his review because he said out loud what many were thinking but would not say to our face.

Ben calls out names and websites of his foes. He focuses on how his family allegedly became victims of spiritual abuse. I warn listeners to take Ben and Kami's bereavement with a grain of salt. While Ben has inspired many with his family endurance challenges, his ultimate endurance challenge has begun: how long can his family wage war with his relatives, former business partners, and previous spiritual mentors.

Coming out about our abuse was the most difficult, honest, and cutting-edge material I had ever published. It took more introspection and honesty than anything I had ever created, making it my best material to date. And yet, not one person came forward and said, "thank you for sharing those facts." Even if we arrived at different conclusions or beliefs, they could not validate our story. My friends of 20 years saw my new material as a betrayal. Like I was now on the other team. My words were only a threat. Jeremiah said my podcast was harmful and disloyal to the family and further proof that I was dangerous. At first, these responses frustrated me. But I could see how they all followed the same pattern as many others who attempted to dismiss us:

- They used vague accusations and never called out specific facts.

- They debase your credibility by referring to vague spiritual infractions and impure motives.

- They come across as loving and pretend to be looking out for our best interests but are really just protecting themselves.

These patterns were easy for me to spot now that I had seen them from so many sources. John's feedback was designed to protect a system he had invested his whole life in and wasn't ready to change. He was willing to sacrifice me, my work, and our friendship to remain unchanged. I had been complicit until the moment I shared. I may have been betraying my old team but for the first time I had stopped betraying myself.

NO CROSS TALK

Loyalty Is Overrated

I had always prided myself in being able to take feedback and keep an open mind. I found glory in taking the high road and killing my haters with kindness. But John's review made me feel differently. It was a weapon used to invalidate my story and sent me into a spiral of doubt and confusion. I was so insecure and unfocused about my creative direction and doubted every creative decision. Writing this now, I can see them for what they are, but when I was going though it, critical comments, especially from people in my old life, paralyzed me.

Even though my audience was tiny and I wasn't making any money, I was still publishing videos five days a week, just because I knew I couldn't live with myself if I didn't. But any negative feedback would send me into mental spirals of doubt that would take hours away from editing or filming. Loyalty to God and my so-called "family" had always been my top priority. Even when they had stabbed me in the back, I felt like I was doing my duty to listen and show up in the relationship. But now I could see the cost, and for the first time in my life, I felt like I had a choice. Instead of being loyal to a nameless group of people who had done everything in their power to silence me and sabotage my endeavors, I would now protect myself and my work.

I decided to implement a rule I learned in the basement: no cross talk. Unless I asked for someone's opinion, I wouldn't allow anyone to give it to me. I would eliminate people who cross-talked without permission. Since many people had stopped seeking me out in person, eliminating these voices took the form of unfollowing, unfriending, unsubscribing and blocking on social media. Yes, they would call me rude. Yes, this would confirm their accusations of pride. But I didn't care. I was done being their bitch.

When Courage Is Walking Away

I always thought that courage was tied to the amount that I sacrificed. When my church friends left, I blamed myself, thinking I should have sacrificed more. I needed a new definition of courage. I could also see that my original dream of being shot down in a plane over Africa, was cowardly. The people who I thought would be begging for me to preach about Jesus and sin, didn't exist.

Then I thought that courage was tied to my level of authenticity. I thought it was my job to be authentic to my community, even when they ignored or shunned me. But, in front of the wrong people, authenticity was a waste, because deep connection was impossible. Courage wasn't *sacrificing* myself for people who didn't value me, it was *walking away* from those relationships.

Ending my Christian relationships felt like throwing away three decades of my life because it's the only place I had invested. So, I told myself that the distance would be temporary. Even though I knew these relationships were dangerous to me, I felt a strong attraction, like a magnet, to these people and dynamics that I was the most comfortable with. I dreamed of a reunion someday where we would go back to the good ol' days. But I could see now that in order to be a part of these relationships, I had put so much of myself behind bars just to fit in. It had almost killed me. Now, I started to believe:

- If "friends" weren't there for me, it's not a healthy relationship for me to be there for them. My therapist called this enablement.

- If people can not celebrate me doing what makes me healthy, they are not my friends.
- For the first time in my life, I had to prioritize the work that was my true calling. If I didn't I would die. I couldn't be a friend to anyone as a corpse.

Finally, I was ready to walk away. This looked like returning a gift card with a harsh note to my in-laws. Yes, it was rude. Yes, it got me uninvited to Thanksgiving, Christmas and everything else. But it was the first time I stood up and spoke my truth in the relationship. I was still stuck thinking of my friend John's scathing review on our podcast. He had more than a million subscribers and I had less than 100. I respected John and wanted his friendship but now I cared about my work more. So, instead of issuing an apology, I recorded a whole podcast explaining John's review as a form of gaslighting. Then I published it. I burned my ships.

me doing what makes me healthy.

Draft 9

Being honest about my abusers had a ripple effect on my work that I didn't anticipate. Honesty begets more honesty and calling bullshit on my old friends made it possible to see my own bullshit. I was five years into studying the hero's journey and storytelling methods and nine drafts into *2000 Miles Together* about our family hiking the Appalachian Trail when I realized I had bullshitted the whole thing. The hero's journey and all popular story models say you need to make the hero suffer. In movies, the protagonist must be down on their luck in the first five minutes or the audience will not relate and cheer for them. In my book, I was the protagonist. But my book told stories of crushing miles, a few rough days but mostly our success by finishing. It made me look like an infallible superhero. I had written an adventure hiking novel. The problem was, the book was boring, even to me. My writing focused on hiking — an aspect of life that wasn't that difficult. I had done this because it's what I thought other people wanted to hear.

Now, I stared at the 90,000 words and asked a new question. What was I the most interested in? What kind of book did I want to read? What was the book I needed? There were hundreds of hiking books about the AT that talked about trees, boots, and bears, and none of them were interesting to me. And when I thought back about our experience, it wasn't the hiking that stood out. The experiences that stood out to me were the times I lost control as a parent.

Rainier, whose birth we had published on YouTube, was two years old when we hiked the trail. I had shared one story on the vlog from the trail about losing my temper and flicking Rainier on the mouth when he was screaming. The story got us reported to CPS and the sheriff showed up and interviewed our kids. I apologized to Rainier but the whole thing was embarrassing and I tried to block it out of my memory. But that wasn't even the darkest moment on trail.

In August, after five months of walking, we were in the final state – Maine, when I pushed my 13-year-old son so hard that he fell face first into the water. This was the son William had told me to hold when he cried. But instead of holding him, I shoved him into a puddle with our two year old on his back. We had never told the story publicly and I had almost forgotten about it. Now, as I mentioned it to Kami, she said that was her lowest point of the entire hike. I had skipped the lowest point of our entire five month journey completely to focus on our success as hikers. This is why the hiking book I had spent 18 months on was boring beyond tears.

I reluctantly called my co-writer, Meghan, and told her the story of the puddle, hoping she might say it was too late. "You HAVE to include that," was her response. Like William had told me back at Whole Foods, if I was going to write a book that really connected and helped others, I needed to talk about the thing I least wanted to talk about — I needed to lead with my weakness and write about pushing my son face first into the puddle. While the thought of losing my reputation once again was scary, I was more scared by living as a prisoner inside walls I had built.

lead with my weakness

A Visit From An Old Friend

Even though I had changed so much internally and felt light-years away from our church friends, we still lived a couple of miles from most of them, shopped at the same grocery stores, and saw them at the same coffee shops. Our kids often came back with stories of hanging out with their friends and I fantasized of rekindling my old friendships, that one of my friends would see how happy I was and ask me how I had changed and things could return to the way they once were.

One night our family was sitting around a fire when my old friend, Mark, and his wife walked into our backyard unannounced. Mark was my blackjack team manager who I had climbed mountains with and who had lived in my home with my children. He was also the one who told me that I had been excommunicated and that he wouldn't speak to me. But it had been four years since then. We sat around awkwardly and no one got up to hug them. And then Mark smiled and handed me a bottle of wine and a bar of chocolate. "We brought these back from Washington for you," he said. It was a peace offering. "Thanks," was all I could muster before they waved and started to walk away. "We don't want to interrupt, we just wanted to say hi and we miss you guys."

Eager to rekindle the connection, I later met Mark at a bar four blocks from my house. He was still wearing his Patagonia hat and Chaco sandals, even though it was winter. He offered me a drink and we lit up some cigars. "We love and miss you guys so much and tell our kids that you're our best friends," he offered. I asked him what had changed that led to him reaching out. He stared back at me blankly.

"We love you guys!" was all he said.

"Then how do you justify how you treated us?" I asked.

"That wouldn't really be appropriate to talk about with you since you chose not to be in the church anymore," he said smugly.

"Well, it wasn't exactly our choice…" I started.

He smirked and looked down over his glasses as if he had caught me. "You were living in sin and you weren't even willing to try and change."

"That's one side of the story," I said, hoping I would finally have my chance to explain what we had actually been through, the six figures we had lost and the side of the story he had never heard. But he cut me off.

"Listen, you're splitting hairs."

My pulse was racing and responses came quickly to my mind as I recalled the dialogues I had been preparing to say for years. But I didn't say anything. I had made a mistake. Mark hadn't changed his perspective of me. He didn't want to hear my side of the story. He had dropped off the gifts to ease his conscience and reinforce his position having the higher ground. Kind of like you would visit your kids after putting them in time-out to remind them that you love them. I was his mission field.

When we said goodbye, there was no handshake or "let's do this again soon." Only walking away.

Over the next few months, my fantasies fueled me to reach out to numerous people from my past to feel out any change or potential for reconnection. I sent a letter apologizing to my in-laws for my rude note. I met a friend from my block, who we had spent six nights a week with, for drinks. I sent a text to a friend thanking him for a Yeti cup that he gave me as a gift that I still used. He texted back:

"I'm sorry to see where you've gone since that Christmas. I feel like you are leading your wife, kids and others down the path to self-destruction. There is still time to turn to God."

My fantasies were just that: a fantasy. Where I hoped for change and reconnection, I found that people had either forgotten about us and moved on with their busy lives or had doubled down on their opinion of me. While I saw my new authenticity as improvement, my old friends saw my life as confirmation that I was going down the wrong track. They patted themselves on the back for cutting me off when they did. To them, I was still learning "the hard way."

The ending of these relationships was hard to accept but I felt like I had the closure I needed and I no longer felt surprised. The more we changed, the more the doors shut to the places and people we used to relate with the best. After meeting Mark, I had a new feeling. I felt sorry for him. Even if I was accepted back, I couldn't imagine returning. The summer after we had celebrated our AT hike, we planned on driving across the country with our family to volunteer in the kitchen at the Bible camp. Ten days before we were ready to leave, I got a phone call. Someone had watched one of our YouTube videos in which we said we no longer believed it was a sin to be gay. He told us we were no longer welcome to cook at camp. Even though we had never told anyone at camp, never tried to convert anyone, and it wasn't even in their explicit rules, it was clear: we were too threatening. The kids cried but I had known it was only a matter of time.

These people and places that I had loved so much were gone and there would never be a glorious reunion. I had changed. When you start sharing honestly for the first time, you will lose everyone that is threatened by your vulnerability. This is inevitable. They may challenge or threaten you to your face or they may quietly disappear. But the same types of creatures that are attracted to a caterpillar are not the same as those who are attracted to a butterfly. I had held myself hostage, wishing for those inside of the church to change their minds and accept me. With my mind no longer focused on lost relationships and feeling rejected, I was able to focus on what I had to offer the world and cultivate something new.

They're Out There

Nature abhors a vacuum and I had been filling mine with garbage. Now that I had space, my sharing started to attract others. I didn't know they were out there!

Instead of trying to shift people's whole moral framework to get them into heaven, now I just started to show people more of our lives. On our vlog, a lot of people liked seeing the inner workings of a family that didn't fit into the neat little boxes society has for them. We had videos of Kami and me smoking cigars, running with the kids, and we were still filming our marital fights. Much of our feedback said the same thing: "just you being you, allows me to be me."

One day I got a DM from an old friend named Katie. At first I was confused because Katie was a part of the community and had lived with some of the leaders that excommunicated me. "Are you willing to go out for a cup of coffee? I think we may have some things in common."

Over coffee, she shared her story. Just like me, Katie had spent her whole life following the rules, trying to please God and obey the wisdom of the leaders. And just like me, it had almost killed her. When she left, the same group that had called her "family" now would not let the kids she had nannied for a decade even speak to her. Like me, she blamed herself.

Over the next six months, many others, like Katie, reached out. Most of these meetings were held in secret because people were worried about what would happen if seen in public. These people were scared, directionless and often crippled relationally and artistically. Cults survived by making the dissenters feel isolated.

Like they were the crazy ones. Like they were impure and didn't have a right to community or a voice. Each of these people said that by hearing our story (most of them listened to the entire ten hour podcast) it made them feel less crazy and most importantly, not alone. Katie and others were still employed by members of the community. To them, speaking out meant losing their job and identity. They thanked me for my courage. It was then that I could see that it wasn't prideful to *share* my story or insights. It was prideful to *keep* my story to myself.

Even though I wasn't focused on changing people's beliefs, many beliefs did change. Rainier's birth video, filmed in the attic, became our most popular video by far, racking up more than 3.5 million views. There were thousands of comments from all parts of the world saying the video was one of the most life-changing videos they'd ever seen. Many said it changed their views on birth, family, and kids.

The same birth process that had horrified Jeremiah and the podcast that he called harmful and disloyal had inspired strangers and saved others. I was discovering people that were attracted to who I actually was and my actual story. This meant I was on my way to building a new tribe. My therapist was wrong. I didn't have an *exaggerated* need for intimacy and expression. I just had an *unmet* need for intimacy and expression. A need that I was never able to meet with friends inside of the church.

Fanatics

Connection

Now that I was sharing my life more openly, I discovered connection in many unexpected places. Remember Andy, my skateboarding friend from high school that came to our first child's birth? While Kami's family had experienced disgust and scandal over Dove's birth experience, Andy had a different experience. Twenty years later, with Dove now an adult, we sat at a Red Robin eating burgers. His appearance had changed. Due to antidepressants, he had gained a lot of weight and he now only wore black. As we sat eating burgers, he shared his perspective of that first birth 20 years earlier. "I was reborn that day," he said. He went on to tell how experiencing Dove's birth had changed the way he saw life, sex, bodies, and God. "I saw a miracle," he said. Then he took off his sweatshirt and showed us his very colorful tattoo that covered his full arm. "That's the story of Jonah," he said. "Jonah means Dove in Hebrew….I never want to forget that day."

When I started sharing the things I needed to hear, at first my audience got smaller. But I noticed I had some fanatics that treated my words and art like it was their lifeline. These people bought my book (that was no longer about hiking) when it came out, left glowing reviews, told their friends and, in Andy's case, got an entirely new framework for life that he has never forgotten. Authentic art polarizes. Not everyone will be a fan. But the more authentic and honest, the more valuable your voice will be to the people who appreciate it.

Andy was born with cerebral palsy and doctors told his mom he would never walk. But when Rainier was six, inspired by our running videos, Andy flew across the country and ran his first marathon with our entire family, something the doctors said would be impossible. He did it because we had shared our lives with him. After finishing the 26 miles, Rainier ran back from the finish line to meet Andy. "It was what I always wanted," Andy said. "<u>To feel included…and part of a family</u>." The same message and lifestyle that scared others away motivated people like Andy to live his life to the fullest. Four human births occur every second of the day. But Dove's birth inspired Andy to use his entire arm to share the story and then finish the most difficult accomplishment of his life 20 years later. Andy's life had changed numerous times because of me sharing, something I was never able to accomplish by preaching. Knowing Andy has made me less lonely. This is why I share.

to feel included & part of a family

Famous

Over the course of the next five years, I achieved a type of fame I never thought possible. Submitting to my schedule of five days a week, I had published more than 1,000 vlog episodes and our channel had grown from 30 to 50,000 subscribers. When my book was released, it made bestseller lists in six categories. Millions of people have heard my story or at least parts of it. My family and projects have been featured on everything from Good Morning America to Perez Hilton and we even got a shoe sponsorship. If popularity or reach is your goal, having the courage to share is a step you should take.

But for me, popularity or limelight was a side effect. The effects and benefits of popularity fizzled out, in some cases literally overnight. The shoe company stopped returning our phone calls and cases of books sit in my dining room. We found new critics. During one news cycle, many critics claimed we were on YouTube just "for the attention" — an accusation that felt oh too familiar. There were some perks that came with fame. Being recognized on the street was fun at first. But being expected to perform or be someone's hero felt very similar to the role I had played in my first 30 years as a Christian leader. I didn't want a new role with a new pedestal. I wanted freedom and I wanted connection.

When Smaller Is Better

Having spent my whole life in our tight-knit, spiritual community, my shift to authenticity was marked for years with one feeling: loss. All I felt was what I had lost. The "lifelong" friends, the family, the lost time and status…. for years I felt like a failure, like I had somehow gone backward.

I lost everything. At least, everything that I knew. But I gained so much more. Instead of fame or blind commitment, I learned a new way to calculate success. It is so much more valuable to have one person – a true fan, friend or lover, desire and appreciate all of who I am, than 100 people just using a role I played to bring them comfort. To the 100 who wanted me to play a role, I was replaceable. But just like I learned in SA, there were now people whose very life depended on me being my authentic self.* I had found some of these people in 12-step groups and some from the vlog. These people had not been scared away with my truth. And when I released *2000 Miles Together*, a book that had transformed from a predictable and boring hiking book to a gritty story of a parent losing control, throwing temper tantrums and yet, still managing to hike, the people who bought and reviewed it were grateful it wasn't a hiking book. They wanted a level of honesty and introspection that they had come to expect from me. They wanted the good *and* the bad. They wanted the crazy angles that only I saw and they appreciated the fact that I slaved for two years over ten drafts to deliver a product I was finally proud of. They didn't call it pride or attention-seeking; they saw it as a gift. But, building any fan base is a double-edged sword.

For a look into the business side of the "smaller is better" phenomenon, check out the 1,000 True Fans essay by Kevin Kelly. He proves that instead of the millions of fans professional artists think they need, an artist can make $100,000 a year from having only 1000 true fans, defined as those who would buy $100 worth of what you create every year.

Even though I was just breaking through to the point where I could make money, I was losing motivation for posting videos on YouTube. I felt like I had found my voice. And the place I was most excited to share wasn't in the basement and it wasn't on the internet or in books. It didn't involve a crowd and it didn't involve likes, sales, reviews or money. The place I was the most excited to share was in my home.

home

share

Full Circle

Back when my SA sponsor, William, asked me to hold my son when he was crying, I was just following directions. I wasn't working toward anything, or so I thought. Back then, what I was able to handle was very limited. I lived my life by how I thought things *should* be. I thought my conscious belief system was what really mattered in life: I was saved, I was a new creation. Everything else I was in denial of. When we had kids, remaining in denial became more difficult. Instead of just shutting up the voices in my head, I had to shut the kids' voices up that came in the form of crying, shouting, and dissenting opinions. We silenced those voices in the name of love and parenting, but really I was afraid. I was afraid of anything that didn't fit into my narrow understanding of reality.

I protected my narrow understanding of reality by ignoring the many people who disappeared in church over the years. I told myself that it was their fault. *They* made bad choices, *they* were rebellious, or *they* walked away. I was in denial and wanted to be special. So hungry to accept the compliments and status, I had ignored all inconvenient evidence around me. William had expanded my threshold by having me hold my crying child instead of trying to stop him or exiling him to his room. He had taught me to have compassion for those that seemed so different than I was and that I was just like those who I thought I was so much better than. And now I could see a different story of those who left the church. Some of the people who disappeared were never *able* to fit in. Instead of accommodating them, the church had pushed them out, blamed and then erased them. I had been a part of this.

I didn't trust the church and I didn't trust the parts of me that isolating judgment came from. In the basement I had worked hard at accepting the types of people society had written off. I listened and heard their stories. The *no cross talk* rule prevented me from judging until eventually I found so much value from listening to outcasts that I stopped feeling the need to judge at all. I could just be present. And then when I found out I could use these skills at home, I brought them there. After a decade of practice, I no longer felt the need to judge. I wanted something more than the illusion of superiority. I didn't need to spew opinions. <u>I wanted connection</u>. <u>I wanted friendship</u>. I wanted to be a good dad to my kids, but not by changing them, by enjoying who they really were.

Our kids' varying actions around drugs, sex, or career gave me every license to examine and critique from my pedestal of power and success. But now, our oldest, Dove, whose birth I started this book with, had turned 21 and moved out. Three of our kids had boyfriends or girlfriends that we wanted to judge but chose instead to accept. Our kids had changed their beliefs, gotten tattoos, and made school and financial choices all different than what I would have done. Each divergence was an opportunity to just listen, accept, and create space without judgment. This was more relaxing, fulfilling and connecting than the judgmental parenting I used to occupy myself with.

In the years that followed, we started to see the fallout of how our parenting would have gone. Our old friends' parenting was getting stricter and stricter, creating more and more rules around driving and dating. They still spent most of their parenting energy preaching their morals. Most of their kids were sneaking around more than ever. They didn't feel safe with their parents. They didn't feel heard. Their codes of purity and religion were preventing them from deep relationships. I no longer felt the need to teach, correct, and judge our kids. I could just listen, be present, and enjoy them.

One day we sat in Arby's as one of our children told us of the thrill of their first sexual experience. Our kid shared their concerns, excitement, and rush of feelings. Because they knew we wouldn't judge them. We would just listen and be there with them. As we dipped curly fries in Arby's sauce it felt natural to just listen. We didn't tell them what they were doing was wrong and we didn't offer any advice. We just shared parts of our story and let them know they were not alone. Five years before, I would have laughed at this possibility.

The child was the same age Kami and I were when we were confused, fighting, and isolated. Now that I had stopped preaching, my child wanted my opinion and my presence, in the exact realm that I had experienced the most loneliness.

Afterward Kami looked at me with the empty Arby's sauce packets on the table.

"I think we're doing something right."

My Masterpiece

Since the age of four, my relationships had been limited by preaching. Preaching told people what I *wanted* to be, not who I really *was*. Right after I got engaged to Kami, at the age of 20, I received a second chance with two secrets I had never told anyone. The first secret was that I struggled with masturbation, a blatant sin in our community. The second was a sexual event that happened with a family member as a child. Both of these things had created shame and defined me as a failure throughout all of my adolescence. I felt like Kami had the right to know so that she could walk away before we tied the knot permanently. It scared me to tell the truth but I had read enough romance novels to know that I wanted the type of relationship where someone would give themself to me fully. The only way to get this was to give *myself* fully and tell the whole truth.

While I didn't mind wearing two faces at church, keeping secrets from my lover seemed harmful to the relationship I dreamed of. We sat on the black leather couch in my parent's house. Finally, I jumped off the cliff. "There's some things I have to tell you…" Three painful and long minutes later I was done. I felt nervous and agitated but I also felt free. Like I had finished my part. And then I waited for the announcement that our relationship was over. That my sins were too much, too bad.

But the disgust and withdrawal never came. Something else was there instead, something I had never experienced before…the feeling that a friend knew everything about me and still wanted me. Wanted me even more than before.

I had no idea how my act of sharing and Kami's acceptance would impact my career, art, and our entire friend groups. I only knew that I wanted to be with her. That relationship, based upon vulnerability, became the backbone that gave me the courage to walk into SA. It gave me the courage to share my sexual inventory with thousands, share about stealing from my best friends on the largest radio show in the country, start a vlog, and keep on sharing even when, especially when, we got excommunicated by our entire community and most of our family.

After that moment on the black leather couch, I knew Kami would never leave me. More importantly, I knew she was deeply attracted to who I was, not what I preached. Later in our relationship, as my comfort in sharing my shadows grew, I also got more comfortable confessing positive things.

One night after 20 years of marriage, while experimenting with molly, a drug most people try in college at raves, I laid in the bed with her and for more than three hours, and told her ways I was thankful for her love and partnership. I wasn't blowing smoke up her ass and it wasn't posturing to show how good our marriage was. It was just sharing my experience of a friend that had stuck with me through thick and thin. We had created a partnership that fit who we actually were, not who we thought the world wanted us to be.

Since then, we have both jumped off of thousands of cliffs, sharing ourselves in the most vulnerable moments. Sharing has been scary and difficult but it has been much more fun than staying safely on the ledge. In building a YouTube channel, a multi-million dollar advertising business, a blackjack team, and finishing my first successful book, my relationship with her is the piece of art I am the most proud of. It's the place I have experienced the most joy and has been the most life-changing. I often think about that first moment on the black leather couch when I didn't know what would happen and I think it was the most courageous and successful accomplishment in my life. It all came from a decision to share.

<u>Worth It</u>

I was in the van driving across the country when I blurted out "I've always wanted to go to a nude beach," to Kami. We had always been taught that our naked bodies were only for each other and we were not to be seen by others. We were supposed to be exclusively satisfied with each other and anything else was cheating. I felt guilty for having fantasies of other people and situations that could ruin our relationship. It was one thing to be honest about hurting someone else. It was a whole other thing to be honest about how our relationship was falling short. But I had learned from so many avenues, "saving my ass or saving my face," "leading with weakness," and "putting my oxygen mask on first," that the best path forward for health and relationships often sacrifices short-term nobility. I had gone without my fantasy for 20 years and could go 20 more. But I felt good because I had shared with her a piece of me.

So I was surprised when she said "thanks for sharing, that sounds like fun and turns me on!" I had thought that by protecting my spouse from my bad desires I was protecting our intimacy. That was a lie. I was protecting the roles that we had played in our relationship. I was being a coward because I couldn't imagine life outside of those roles.

Three years later, Kami came out with her own confession. We were at the fanciest steakhouse in town and it was her birthday. "I'm gay," she said. "I'm not sure if I'm bi or pansexual or non-binary but I've felt different my whole life."

At first this was the scariest thing I'd ever heard — like she wanted to move on, like I wasn't measuring up. The next week she took off her wedding ring. "It just feels like the right thing for me, right now," she said. What did this mean for our marriage? For me? We had a certain dynamic that worked and now it felt like with our openness, maybe we had gone too far. This is what Jeremiah had warned me about. But while I valued the time that we had had together and the role that she had played in my life, I had learned to value her for who she was, more. And instead of trying to make me happy, or fulfill a role, in her birthday confession she had offered me a piece of herself. She had been generous with me in a way she never had, in a way she had never offered anyone. By me sharing my life, Kami had felt safe enough to share hers.

She had accepted me when I confessed on the couch before we got married and when I told her how hard our life was going to be following Jesus when I proposed, and then again when we had walked away from our entire community. Now it was my turn to accept her.

The next morning we sat around the kitchen table, her wedding ring on the nightstand in the other room. I said, "I will love and support you no matter what and will help you explore anything you need in any way I can." We both had tears in our eyes.

When I increased my capacity to share my life, it increased my capacity to accept others. This in turn increased the capacity of those around me to accept themselves and expand their potential. Kami started to accept her own sexual desires instead of just trying to satisfy mine. With my lead, she started to accept parts of herself that had been suppressed since childhood and share more and more things that neither of us could have imagined. Instead of being the sidekick, she started to show up as a partner and friend, sharing parts of herself we didn't know existed. The next few years opened up a whirlwind of increased vulnerability, wilder sex, new roles played with each other, and multiple nude beaches. Where before I had always been the leader, the comforter, the one with the ideas and the power, now we were taking turns. Now she held *me* and comforted *me*. These experiences showed me that I didn't want safety. I didn't want rigid roles. I wanted a partner. I wanted a friend. I wanted connection. And the way we stayed connected through it all was with a commitment to share, no matter how weird, awkward, or dangerous.

Just like we had learned in every other situation, love and intimacy are so much more wild and fun when the person you're with takes that risk and shares themself. We had long since broken the rules and etiquette our marriage started with. Not because we didn't care about each other, but because we cared about each other more than the roles of marriage allowed. As we went around sampling the different sins that we had resisted for so long, we found it was never really the sins we wanted. It was connection. Our previous sex life required replaying unfulfilled porn fantasies in our heads but in helping each other live out our fantasies we realized it was really each other that we wanted. By having strict purity codes and arbitrary boundaries, we were really closing off parts of ourselves and each other that we were afraid of. Breaking the rules gave us new opportunities to explore and accept each other much more deeply than when we just affirmed how much the other's beliefs validated our own. We both learned if someone really wants connection with you, they will appreciate hearing what honestly turns you on. If they don't appreciate it, it's not you they want to be connected to. They're just using you for a feeling of safety and security — a role that can easily be replaced. With each other, we have found the beauty underneath is so much more rare, intriguing and captivating than the shallow roles we were taught to play. Every morning we sit around the kitchen table and share our feelings, our goals, and ourselves with each other and it is the highlight of my day.

Many people are stingy with sharing themselves. For good reason. They have been hurt. They have been burned or penalized for sharing. So they have given up. They have resorted to the much safer path of preaching. Maybe they post their ideas on social media or maybe the ideas are just looped in their own head, preaching to themselves. I understand why. When you share it is scary. There's a reason people don't do it. But I have learned that there's more to people than the ideas we preach. We are not here to provide safety to institutions or play a replaceable role. We are human. We are lovers. For true connection to happen, we need tools and motives that go beyond preaching. We need the feelings. We need the frustrations. We need the failures. And we need the radical acceptance that can only come from sharing.

I have preached and shared to the extreme. I have made bestseller lists, news headlines, and reached the depths of my lover's heart. I have also lost my dignity, my community, and my reputation in the process. The entire point of this book is to show you that for me, it was worth it. Connection has been better than the respect I received from everyone I thought was important. Although it felt safer to inspire others with my ideas, I learned that this didn't allow me to change. Change was natural. And intimacy allowed change because it was based on someone being attracted to me, not just my ideas.

I have committed to sacrificing my ideas and dignity to connect with myself, Kami, and others. I won't cling to roles or suppress my truth. I will continue to be brave in honestly sharing myself with Kami, my kids and the world. I don't know what sharing will look like for you. All I know is that if your journey is anything like mine, I think it will be worth it for you, too.

partner
friend
connection

Appendix

Put your oxygen mask on first.

Recipe For Sharing

This book was intended as a "self-help" book before a friend told me I was actually writing a love story. For those looking for specific actionable steps, here are some suggestions for implementing this material into your own life:

Lead With Your Weakness
The thing that you are the most afraid of, that you are the most embarrassed by, is actually your strongest material to work with. It's what makes you you and it's what will help connect you with others that can assist in your healing and be your new support system. It may seem scary. Good. That's how you know you're getting to the good stuff.

Filter Further
If you are unable to lead with your weakness, there's a good chance you are surrounded by the wrong people. Maybe they were the right people up until this point but that doesn't matter. You need to surround yourself with the people who will support you with the type of person you want to become. Don't waste your time and energy trying to change anyone's mind. Be ruthless. Unfollow, block, tell people you're busy. Whatever it takes to protect your sacred calling. Put your oxygen mask on first. It's the best thing you can do for those you love.

Share more

Share your art, share your words, share yourself. Share more with a friend, a lover, or with yourself in a journal. It seems unintuitive to lean into the area that hurt you but it's in this same place that you will find health. Sharing yourself is the only way to grow beyond the events that hurt you to find long-term support, companionship and strength. It makes the world a better place. It will make you a better person. Sharing operates off of hope. You might not have any. Sharing is how you get it back. Don't know where to start? Can I offer a suggestion borrowed from William? Start with the thing you least want to talk about. If that sounds too heavy-duty, here are some other ideas:

- A favorite memory with a parent
- A letter to a friend about what you appreciate
- A nude/sext to a lover
- A shitty (or positive) experience with a restaurant owner
- A hidden desire with a loved one
- A secret
- How you're proud of a child
- An addiction
- A dream you've always had
- A goal for this next week/month/year
- What makes you the most angry
- One of those stupid facebook get to know me lists
- Your biggest failure
- Your greatest accomplishment
- A sexual fantasy
- A business idea

Literally anything because the point is not what you're sharing. The point is that you are sharing with the world more of yourself.

This book was a labor of love and I am thankful to share it with **YOU**! I would love to hear **YOUR** thoughts/stories/reactions.

You can msg me direct _or_ if you want to help me you can post a review on amazon, audible, or goodreads so others can hear your thoughts as well (I will read it too). If there is anyone specific you think would benefit from this message I would appreciate you letting them know that this book exists. Thanks! -Ben

Resources

In the podcast about cults there is a list of eight prevalent indicators of brainwashing. That list is taken from a book titled Thought Reform and the Psychology of Totalism by Robert Jay Lifton. This is the list taken from the book's Wikipedia page.

Eight Criteria for Thought Reform:
1. **Milieu Control**. The group or its leaders controls information and communication both within the environment and, ultimately, within the individual, resulting in a significant degree of isolation from society at large.
2. **Mystical Manipulation**. The group manipulates experiences that appear spontaneous to demonstrate divine authority, spiritual advancement, or some exceptional talent or insight that sets the leader and/or group apart from humanity, and that allows a reinterpretation of historical events, scripture, and other experiences. Coincidences and happenstance oddities are interpreted as omens or prophecies.
3. **Demand for Purity**. The group constantly exhorts members to view the world as black and white, conform to the group ideology, and strive for perfection. The induction of guilt and/or shame is a powerful control device used here.
4. **Confession**. The group defines sins that members should confess either to a personal monitor or publicly to the group. There is no confidentiality; the leaders discuss and exploit members' "sins," "attitudes," and "faults".
5. **Sacred Science**. The group's doctrine or ideology is considered to be the ultimate Truth, beyond all questioning or dispute. Truth is not to be found outside the group. The leader, as the spokesperson for God or all humanity, is likewise above criticism.

6. **Loading the Language.** The group interprets or uses words and phrases in new ways so that often the outside world does not understand. This jargon consists of thought-terminating clichés, which serve to alter members' thought processes to conform to the group's way of thinking.
7. **Doctrine over person.** Members' personal experiences are subordinate to the sacred science; members must deny or reinterpret any contrary experiences to fit the group ideology.
8. **Dispensing of existence.** The group has the prerogative to decide who has the right to exist and who does not. This is usually not literal but means that those in the outside world are not saved, unenlightened, unconscious, and must be converted to the group's ideology. If they do not join the group or are critical of the group, then they must be rejected by the members. Thus, the outside world loses all credibility. In conjunction, should any member leave the group, he or she must be rejected also.

Acknowledgements

Tim, Carrie, Robin, Anya, Caleb, Amy, Dirk, Paulina, Meghan, Hal, Kami for taking the time to read and provide feedback and encouragement. Thanks to Amy Vos for reaching out and helping with the editing. This book would not have the capitalization or commas it deserves without your help.

And a very special thanks to David Danelo who had the courage to share with me that I was writing the wrong book. On a voice note he said, "I don't think you have a book about Christian storytelling. I think you have a book called the Share. It's a love story. I'll tell you more." You were right.

Ben Crawford, author of the bestselling book "2000 Miles Together: The Story of the Largest Family to Hike the Appalachian Trail," has been featured on Good Morning America and NPR's "This American Life." Formerly entrenched in fundamentalist religion and at the helm of one of the globe's largest blackjack teams, spotlighted in the documentary "Holy Rollers: The True Story of Card Counting Christians," Crawford boasts a tapestry of experiences. Retired in his 30s, he's a prolific YouTuber with over 1000 uploads and finds solace in poker and marathon running with his six children.

Instagram
@3enCrawford
@fightfortogether

Made in United States
Troutdale, OR
07/12/2024